Africa's Challenge to America

AFRICA'S
Challenge to
AMERICA

By Chester Bowles

FOREWORD BY THOMAS K. FINLETTER

NEGRO UNIVERSITIES PRESS
WESTPORT, CONNECTICUT

Foreword

In the first phase of our foreign policy after World War II, as we found ourselves driven more and more into major responsibility for the affairs of the free world, our attention was concentrated on what became known as the NATO area. Our problem here was to prepare our defenses against our former ally, Russia, which, as soon as the fighting of World War II was over, renewed its efforts to conquer the world.

The problem of the defense of Western society was made easier by our common heritage and by our equally common determination that we did not intend to be conquered by Russia. Wise measures prepared the groundwork for the pooling of our defenses against the Russians. The Marshall Plan restored the economic strength of war-battered Europe; the North Atlantic Treaty provided the juridical basis for the common defense; and then the North Atlantic Defense Force gave us the military means of making clear to Russia that we did not intend to be defeated or overawed by the massive Red Army and the growing Russian air-atomic power.

The United States worked well with its partners of Western society in developing a common front of economic well-being and self-defense in the NATO area. But what about the rest of the world, the whole vast line of contact between freedom and communism from Turkey eastward to the Near East, South Asia, Southeast Asia, China, Japan, and on to the Aleutians? How was this part of the world to be defended against the Communist plan of conquest? For surely this vast area could not be lost to communism without imperiling the homeland of Western society itself.

At first there were heavy defeats for freedom in this vast world outside Western society. The great citadel of China fell to communism. Now the Russians had a powerful partner in the East to work toward the conquest of the rest of the world that was still free. What was to be our formula for resistance in this enormous area?

The United States attempted to accomplish in the area *outside* NATO what had succeeded *within* NATO, namely, to create political-military defenses against expanding communism. The Russian-Chinese partnership gave us some reason for thinking this was the right formula; their first drive was military; they were not subtle about the way they attacked Korea.

We all know how for the first time the principle of collective action for peace was enforced by the United Nations and how the Communist military drive was defeated—in the name of collective action for peace and under the banner of justice and law.

After the war in Korea the Communist partnership became more subtle. There have been no more open invasions since then. We have had the skillful use of Communist cells in those parts of the world the Communists wish to take over, and the support of indigenous movements of revolt such as the Vietminh in Southeast Asia. This was still violence but it was of a new kind. Finally the new offensive of the Russians was launched, with their traveling agents, Marshal Bulganin and Mr. Khrushchev, who attempt to conquer the minds of the indigenous peoples by talking of peace and prosperity.

The latest Russian-Chinese policy is the most dangerous of all because it seeks to ally itself with and to harness the anticolonial revolution which long has been seething and now is active in all formerly colonized countries from China to Morocco.

The anticolonial revolution is based on our traditionally American principles—the principles which make men want to govern themselves and to be free of domination by outsiders. This is not to say that the peoples of Asia, the Near East, and Africa took over this idea from us; but rather, that the urge to freedom is in every man because he is a man. Nevertheless, because of our own origins, we Americans have an identification with the former colonial peoples in their will to freedom.

The fact is, however, that American foreign policy has failed to adapt itself to the anticolonial revolution and thus has been false to its own traditions. We have continued to try to combat the expansion of communism by military alliances and by making military threats from the Formosa Strait to the Northern Tier of Turkey, Iraq, Iran, and Pakistan. Our foreign policy has failed to recognize that if all these vast uncommitted areas are to remain on the side of freedom we ourselves must stand by the principles of freedom and must create a foreign policy which respects the will of these peoples to be as free as we are.

Chester Bowles' great contribution has been that he is the leader of American opinion who has most clearly recognized these basic truisms and has long urged our government to give heed to these irresistible forces of right and freedom.

vii

As early as April, 1942, Mr. Bowles proposed that President Roosevelt and Prime Minister Churchill (or if Churchill would not accede, President Roosevelt alone) expand the Atlantic Charter to include the colonial areas of Africa and Asia.

In a speech delivered in Cleveland on January 25, 1947, Mr. Bowles pointed out the stake the United States has in the political stability of the underdeveloped areas from Japan through Africa and South America. In this speech he proposed that the United States invest one per cent of its gross national product annually through the United Nations in a program abroad for economic development to help assure this stability.

Between 1947 and 1951, before Mr. Bowles went to India as our ambassador, he wrote a score of articles in which he continued to stress the need for economic development of the underdeveloped areas and the danger of depending too much upon a purely military answer to the threats of communism in these areas.

A year before Stalin's death, in January, 1952, Mr. Bowles argued before the Senate Foreign Relations Committee that a new and more formidable Soviet approach to the underdeveloped nations was in the making and that the United States should seize the initiative while time was still on our side.

Shortly after Stalin's death Chester Bowles stated: "There are disturbing signs that Moscow's indifference to the political possibilities of economic assistance to the non-Communist nations of Asia may be changing and a new period of ruble diplomacy lies abroad. . . . A devastatingly effective Soviet version of Point Four could be put together for less than one-fourth of the present $8 billion annual increase in Russia's annual income. The possibilities of such a move on the part of Moscow are sobering to contemplate. If we continue to put our exclusive faith in military negation, we will lose our big chance."

In the fall of 1953 when the United States–Pakistan arms agreement was under consideration Mr. Bowles again warned that our focus on short-term military considerations in this area was likely to give us not more security, but less. He pointed out specifically that such an agreement would upset the delicate balance of power between Pakistan, Afghanistan, and India, further damage our already uneasy relations with India on whose economic and political stability the non-Communist cause in Asia largely depends, and offer the Soviet Union an ideal opportunity for the economic and political penetration of Afghanistan.

On December 19, 1953, he wrote prophetically: "A substantial offer of Soviet economic aid to bolster India's Five Year Plan will almost certainly follow, and we will surely be faced with an all-out Soviet attempt to dominate and infiltrate Afghanistan."

Chester Bowles thus has long been saying that American foreign policy should look back to its own traditional belief in the rights of self-determination and of self-government as a guide for its policy toward the underdeveloped areas of the world. He expressed these views in his book *Ambassador's Report* written after his retirement as United States ambassador to India and in the sequel which appeared in 1955, entitled *The New Dimensions of Peace*. These books dealt mainly with India, the Far East, and the Near East.

Now Chester Bowles presents this new book based on a series of lectures delivered at the University of California in March, 1956, which give his penetrating analysis of the problems of Africa and his suggestions for a new foreign policy for the United States directed to that often-neglected continent.

It is an extension of the analysis that has proved so right in Asia and in the Near East. It is a major contribution to current thinking about American foreign policy.

THOMAS K. FINLETTER

May, 1956

Contents

xi

I

Voices of Africa

In 1945 most Americans looked on Africa, when they thought about it at all, as an exotic and remote land of missionaries, "natives," and big-game hunters, where our interests, happily enough, seemed strictly limited.

In the last few years these impressions have been challenged. The stream of visiting journalists, novelists, social scientists, businessmen, and public officials who return to write and speak of Africa's infinite complexity, wealth, and promise grows steadily larger and more clamorous. Africa can no longer be ignored.

By now most of us have come to realize that Africa covers one-fifth of the earth's surface, an area considerably bigger than China, India, and the United States combined; that Africa has a population of about 200,-000,000 people; that Africa is the richest untapped source of mineral wealth still available to a world that is rapidly devouring its resources; and that large sections of Africa are being torn by a wave of anticolonial nationalism which is creating political problems with a revolutionary potential second only to that of Asia.

I shall not attempt to offer new statistics, new facts, or even new interpretations of this complex continent. My purpose is to discuss, with considerable humility, a subject that has been scarcely touched—America's relationship to Africa against the background of the world struggle. My observations of the current African scene will be limited to what is pertinent to this objective.

A study of Africa is likely to lead the thorough student to the Library of Congress where he will find an excellent guide to background reading prepared in 1952. But before he gets past the title page of *Introduction to Africa* a profoundly important fact about Africa will have been underscored: the guide was prepared by the *European* Affairs Division of the Library of Congress, because the principal political and economic decisions involving three-fourths of Africa's people and nearly three-fourths of its land area are made in London, Paris, Lisbon, and Brussels. Only Ethiopia, Liberia, Libya, Sudan, the Union of South Africa and Egypt (which considers itself part of the Middle East) are now independent of European rule.

French Africa, covering an area twenty times larger than France and with a population that is roughly equal, includes Morocco, Tunisia, Algeria, Madagascar, French Equatorial Africa, French West Africa, the French Camerouns, and French Togoland.

British Africa, with a land area which is also some twenty times larger than the United Kingdom and with a population of 63,000,000, includes the Gold Coast, Sierra Leone, Nigeria, Kenya, Uganda, Basutoland,

2

Bechuanaland, Swaziland, Gambia, Tanganyika, Nyasaland, Southern and Northern Rhodesia, Zanzibar, British Somaliland, British Togoland, and the British Camerouns.

Belgian Africa, which consists of the Congo and the United Nations trust colony of Ruanda-Urundi, has a land area nearly one hundred times that of Belgium. Its population totals 12,000,000.

Portuguese Africa, consisting of Angola and Portuguese Guinea on the Atlantic Ocean, and Mozambique on the Indian Ocean, has a land area twenty-one times that of Portugal. Its total population of 9,500,000 is slightly larger than that of Portugal.

Even Spanish Morocco, one of the smallest colonial areas in Africa with 1,800,000 people, is as big as New Jersey.

As late as 1947 India, Pakistan, Ceylon, Burma, Indochina and Indonesia, with nearly half the population of Asia, were under similar control from European colonial capitals. Except for Indochina, their transition to self-government was largely peaceful. Will the same general pattern hold for Africa where independence by one means or another is almost certainly in the cards? Will America's role be a constructive one? The answers to these questions are by no means assured.

Our slowness in recognizing the political and economic forces which have been turning Asia upside down has already alarmingly reduced American prestige and influence between Cairo and Saigon. If we are to avoid similar failures between Tunis and Capetown, we will need to approach colonial Africa as a crucially important continent with its own problems and its own promise, not as a mosaic of appendages to imperial Europe.

Wealth and power have inescapably committed the United States to world policies and world responsibilities.

To manage them with even a bare adequacy, we can no longer afford to look at any part of this interrelated world through other people's glasses. Indeed, we must hope that not only Americans, but all of the Atlantic peoples will come to understand the full scope of the African challenge and to encourage their governments to adopt positive and realistic policies while there is time and room for maneuver.

As we approach this discussion of American policy toward Africa, a warning seems in order: foreign observers often charge Americans with an oversimplified approach to international affairs. Our practice, they say, is to sum up even the most complex situations in cliches, decide that one side is hopelessly wrong and the other everlastingly right, and then insist on a quick, absolute solution.

In Africa it is particularly important for us to disprove this charge. The answers there, when indeed they can be found at all, will usually be difficult, obscure, and controversial. For instance, those whose dedication to the goal of self-determination leads them to believe that all of Africa's colonies and protectorates can suddenly cut their ties with Europe and emerge as democratic, viable states, are certainly in error. So are those who argue that in the foreseeable future Africans are generally incapable of self-government, and that even though the opposite were the case, we cannot risk the displeasure of our NATO allies by saying so.

When I first visited North Africa as a casual tourist in the 1930's, American isolation—not only from Africa, but also from Europe—was considered feasible, and the Africans, at least, were equally unconcerned about us. When I returned to West, Central, and East Africa in 1955, the situation had drastically changed. My deepest impression then was of the interdependence not only of Africa with Europe, but with Asia and America as well.

4

A LOGICAL STARTING PLACE FOR AN ANALYSIS OF AMERICA'S role in helping to shape Africa's economic and political development is an examination of the contrasting views held in Africa itself about Africa and Africa's relations with the world. Many of the viewpoints which I shall present are emotional and some are founded more on prejudice than on fact. Yet each is earnestly held. Although each is also authentic, I have no intention of imputing them to particular individuals, official or unofficial.

Let us begin our impression-gathering tour with colonial Africa, and because more of Africa's millions live under British rule than under any other, we shall start with some voices from the British colonies.

For the most part the British administrative record in Africa, as in colonial India, Burma, and Ceylon, has been outstanding. Reflecting long experience and a nice sense of compromise, the ties which hold the British possessions, colonies, protectorates, trust colonies and dominions to the Crown are ingeniously flexible.

There are colonies in the classic tradition such as Kenya, and colonies on the verge of dominionhood such as the Gold Coast and Nigeria. Uganda is a protectorate, while Zanzibar is a sultanate under British protection. The Central African Federation comprising Southern Rhodesia, Northern Rhodesia, and Nyasaland defies any definition at all. The Union of South Africa is a full-fledged dominion which at times has appeared to be on the verge of retiring from dominionhood. The Sudan was a condominium which the British shared rather unequally with Egypt, and which has recently achieved full independence.

There are also the British-administered United Nations trust territories of which the largest is the former German colony now called Tanganyika. Another former German colony, South-West Africa, could have become a United

Nations trust territory of the Union of South Africa, but the Union refuses to recognize the United Nations's claims and has all but annexed it.

The ablest of the British administrators in this extraordinary conglomeration of geographical and political entities are pragmatic, tough-minded, and philosophical. Their experience on the colonial firing line has enabled them to take in their stride changes that make Colonel Blimp in his London club apoplectic.

Let us see what a high British official in West Africa has to say:

"When I first came to Africa we had two simple tasks: to maintain law and order, and collect taxes. But what a change we have seen since the war! Today by far the greatest part of our time is spent increasing food production, digging wells, stamping out sleeping sickness, building roads, and putting up primary schools.

"The cynical chaps will tell you that if we didn't do these constructive things we could no longer maintain order and collect taxes. That isn't really quite fair, is it?

"I'll grant that we British have profited handsomely from our West African possessions. But the Africans have profited even more. Just tell me which are the two most illiterate, poverty-stricken, disease-ridden countries in all Africa today? Are they our British colonies, or the French, or Belgian, or even the Portuguese? Not at all; they are the only two independent African nations which have never been colonies—Liberia and Ethiopia.

"British rule in West Africa has sometimes been harsh, perhaps unnecessarily so. But we're not wanton oppressors. Slavery, for instance, wasn't brought to Africa by us. We *found* it here, established centuries ago by the Africans, and we stamped it out at considerable expense. What we *did* bring was respect for freedom, at least as an objective—and in Africa that was something very new.

"You might even say that we helped create the nationalist movements which now challenge us. The young Africans who try to undermine us were educated in British and American universities. You see, we prefer an educated, responsible opposition that knows how to play the game decently.

"In Asia the old British Empire is now largely gone. Malaya, North Borneo, Sarawak, Hong Kong and Singapore are all we have left out there, and Malaya and Singapore will have the responsibility for their own affairs soon. When we promise to grant self-government, as soon as they are ready, to our remaining colonies, not only in Asia but in Africa, even Moscow knows we mean it. The Gold Coast and Nigeria here in British West Africa are close to independence right now."

THE KNOWLEDGE THAT INDEPENDENCE IS JUST AROUND the corner is a heady thing. In the Gold Coast where 4,000,000 Africans stand on the threshold of freedom, we find pride and exhilaration, but also a sober appreciation of the divisive problems that go with self-government. An African member of the Gold Coast government who heads a department in which African and British civil servants work harmoniously side by side speaks with measured optimism.

"We West Africans are an example of enlightened British colonial policy. Here in the Gold Coast, which we shall call Ghana, we have an African prime minister, Kwame Nkrumah, who was educated in America. He has an eleven-man all-African cabinet. Our all-African parliament of 104 members was elected by universal suffrage, and even contains a woman member. Like the Nigerian parliament, it is modeled on the British House of Commons. After we gain full independence it will continue as our governing body. Then, of course, we shall join the British Commonwealth.

"Here in British West Africa you will find an able, well-educated and youthful African leadership, a comparatively high percentage of intellectuals and professional men, and a growing middle class. The law specifically prevents Europeans from owning land, so there are none of the bitter racial conflicts that you'll find in British East Africa. Because we produce more than half the world's cocoa, we have a sizeable amount of foreign exchange. There are also large reserves of manganese and bauxite and ample water power with which to develop our country industrially.

"Even with these advantages, we know that independence will open up formidable problems. Sectional, religious, and tribal differences, for instance, could split Nigeria dangerously. Here in the Gold Coast the powerful Ashanti are demanding regional autonomy, feelings run high and there could be bloodshed. Before the British finally give up their authority we must go through another national election.

"So, as you see, we are the most critical testing ground of democratic self-government in Africa. Our success will encourage orderly progress toward freedom everywhere. Our failure will be a disheartening setback. Europeans who believe that Africans are incapable of self-government will insist that we have proved their point; Africans who believe that a violent upheaval is the only effective way to end white rule will argue that we have proved theirs.

"People in America and Europe who are looking for a peaceful, orderly, democratic solution of the colonial problem have a big stake in our success. We hope they understand it. The help of your government, your foundations, your educators, your businessmen may even be the margin of that success."

WHEN WE JOURNEY INTO BRITISH EAST AND CENTRAL Africa we leave behind the soaring hopefulness of the Gold Coast and Nigeria and encounter an area of varied tensions and uneven progress. The land is high and much of it is fertile; the climate is moderate and healthful all year. As a direct result, we find the economic and political structure complicated by the presence of many Europeans who look on Africa as their permanent home.

Of the 35,000,000 people who live in the Gold Coast and Nigeria only 15,000 are Europeans. Because there is almost no competition with the Africans racial relations are excellent. In Uganda where the numerically weak Europeans own only one per cent of the land, good progress is also being made. In Nyasaland and Tanganyika the number of the European settlers is also small, although they have managed to gain a somewhat stronger voice in the government and in economic affairs.

In Kenya and Southern Rhodesia we find the problem of land competition most acute. Through their ownership of most of the best land, 150,000 Europeans in these two colonies have gained a position of almost total economic dominance over 8,000,000 Africans. These Europeans consider themselves frontiersmen pledged to open up a backward country and entitled by moral right to exploit its resources as they wish. Let us consider the view of a rather typical European settler living in Kenya.

"I came to Kenya in 1919 after fighting for four years in France. I was looking for a new life and I have found it here. Taxes are low, living is cheap, the climate is nearly ideal, and I now own 5,000 acres of good land in these beautiful highlands. I intend to keep that land—*all* of it.

"Even the *good* Africans with whom we deal are no more than children. When the first white settlers came here only three generations ago the natives were more backward than the Britons whom Caesar subdued in England more than 2,000 years ago. They didn't even know the principle of the wheel. They are still savages at heart. Even cannibalism isn't really dead.

"This Mau Mau affair illustrates my point. No European old enough to handle a revolver dares be without one—even in his own home. They've killed nearly forty of us, and the most horrible murders of all have been committed by Kikuyu servants whom their victims were stupid enough to trust. They've also killed over 4,000 of their own people whom they suspected of being on our side.

"These Colonial Office chaps say we've got to bring Africans and Indians into the government and give them more and more responsibilities. That's dangerous nonsense. Give the African a bit of power and the white man will soon be finished.

"The one way to deal with this barbarism is ruthless suppression. It has worked in the past and it will work again. I've handled Africans in my own way for years and I've had no trouble at all."

BLIND REACTION OF THIS KIND IS BALANCED BY A LONGER view, taken by more sober Europeans. Limited participation of Africans and Indians in the Kenya government is supported not only by the British Colonial Office, but by thoughtful new leaders who have emerged from among the settlers. A European minister in the Kenya government puts it this way:

"Let's get one thing clear. Tough talk won't solve our problems. Understand now: we have the military power to wipe out the Mau Mau and we're doing exactly that. But still we Europeans will be pushed out eventually unless we develop a true partnership with the Africans.

"Political reform is a first step, but it's only a beginning. The heart of the present conflict really lies in the land. Most Africans know very little about political rights but they all understand and love the land.

"The 16,000 square miles of cool, healthful, fertile highlands, bigger than either Belgium or the Netherlands, have been reserved for 20,000 Europeans. Most of the 5,000,000 Blacks have

11

been confined to the rocky soil of the reservations where they have learned to distrust and to hate us Europeans. This land conflict is at the heart of our troubles."

MANY ANTHROPOLOGISTS WHO HAVE STUDIED THE COM-plex structure of African society agree that land ownership is crucially important, but suggest that the problem has even more explosive dimensions. Here is one explanation:

"Before the white man came to East Africa the tribal societies provided a sense of security that was physical as well as psychological. These old patterns have now been broken down and the Mau Mau is one particularly ugly result.

"Europeans brought discredit on the old African way of life and induced African leaders to reject the customs, rites, and rituals through which their forefathers had achieved a sense of balance with the spiritual and material world in which they lived.

"Then having destroyed the traditional framework of the African's security, the European through his color bar and his land laws denied Africans access to his own Western institutions where they might have found a new sense of belonging. Frustrated in their dealings with the white man, the Africans have been building up an explosive, inner bitterness which in the Mau Mau revolt broke loose in an orgy of hatred and violence against those who had destroyed their gods and left them empty and alone.

"Few white men bothered to give the Kikuyu a

12

sense of dignity, to understand his frustration, much less to wonder what he was thinking. His apparent subservience was accepted as further evidence of African inferiority and European power.

"Sometimes it seems as though the European, and the American, too, have become incapable of seeing the new world in which we live through the eyes and minds of others. Unless they learn soon, history will ultimately pass them by."

BRITISH EAST AFRICA IS GREATLY AFFECTED BY NEHRU'S India. There are two reasons for this: first, more than half a million Indians live in British East Africa and in South and Central Africa; second, India is hailed by educated Africans as the most effective democratic supporter of their struggle for racial equality and independence from colonial rule. The tested organization and tactics of the Indian National Congress have become the model for many nationalist groups throughout Africa.

Many of the young British-educated African elite are now losing faith not only in Britain but in America, and looking with increasing hope to Cairo and New Delhi. Some of them are looking beyond these capitals of non-involvement to Moscow and Peking. Here is a view which will be heard throughout much of East and Central Africa.

"There are plenty of liberal-minded British in the United Kingdom who know what must be done if self-government is to evolve in an orderly way here in East Africa. But it's the *officials* in London who really count, and few of them dare take a firm position for fear of offending the Europeans who live here. When the Kenya government outlaws the democratically oriented Kenya African Congress there is scarcely a protest.

"There are many sympathetic Americans, too. But for all its talk about democracy and freedom, the United States government thinks it must keep silent to avoid trouble with its NATO allies who still control three-fourths of Africa.

"So we come hard up against one fact: the only non-Communist people who sincerely champion the cause of racial equality and independence in Africa are the new leaders of independent Asia— men like Nehru, Nasser, and U Nu. We can count on them always to speak up for us in the United Nations and elsewhere, and we are grateful. Of course, the Soviet bloc also supports us—for its own cynical reasons. But when Bulganin says 'We hold that colonial regimes are a disgrace to present-day mankind and incompatible with the peaceful and democratic principles of the United Nations' we are nonetheless pleased.

"If Moscow gets control of the nationalist movements in Africa it will be a tragedy. Yet that's bound to happen sooner or later unless the colonial powers come to terms with those of us who understand and want democracy."

The indians and pakistanis themselves who live in East, Central and South Africa face formidable obstacles, not only in their dealings with the Europeans, but often with the Africans. Most of their parents and grandparents were brought to Africa as railway laborers or indentured servants, and today they live in a kind of limbo between the dominant Whites and the subject Blacks. In the Union of South Africa, where they share the ignominy of *apartheid*, they are moving toward political unity with the Africans.

In British East Africa, their position is both more complex and more important. In Kenya, for example, there are three Indians for every European. The Indians largely control retail trade, are prominent in the professions, and provide the bulk of white-collar workers and artisans. An Indian merchant in Nairobi has this to say:

"Here we are not as badly off as the Asians in South Africa, but we are discriminated against and mistrusted. Jawaharlal Nehru said to us frankly, 'You Indians in Africa will not get any support from the government of India in any claim you may advance against the Africans. You are their guests. If you cannot get on there, pack up and go. We will not protect you.'

"This is good advice and we accept it wholeheartedly. We're anxious to help create a better atmosphere. We deplore the Mau Mau excesses. As a matter of fact, they've killed more Asians than Europeans.

"If the Europeans and Africans would let us, we Indians and Pakistanis could provide a bridge between them, but they won't let us. Europeans oppose us because they know our relationship with the Africans is steadily improving, and that we are helping to break down barriers they want kept intact. African resentment toward us dies slowly, too. We've worked hard to become successful merchants, doctors, schoolteachers, bankers. Like any tradesmen in a poor country, we must expect to be mistrusted, but the Europeans

15

make it worse by constantly poisoning the minds of the Africans. I find it hard to be optimistic about the outlook."

THROUGHOUT EAST AND CENTRAL AFRICA THE INCOME of the African worker is a fraction of that of the European. In the copper belt of Northern Rhodesia, which produces 20 per cent of the world's copper, the average income disparity is about twenty-two to one. It is true that the Europeans do more skilled work than the Africans, but the wage differential for similar work in an American mine would be more like two to one. Enlightened Europeans such as this mine manager know how easily this situation could get out of hand:

"The differences in income simply must be narrowed. We must train Africans for the more skilled jobs, pay them a higher share of their wages in cash, and give them more responsibility for the operation of their housing, schools, and services.

"And here's another thing: if the African miners moved up the wage and job scale, gradually pushing most of the Europeans out, these mines would be far more profitable. Now we are forced to pay our European miners in Africa substantially more than the customary wages in the American copper mines, benefits are far more generous, and living costs are no more than half. This inflates our payroll, puts a ceiling on the progress of the Africans, and sets one racial group against the other.

"But the European trade unions resist every proposal that reduces their influence, and we can't yet make a go of it without them. They see every lowering of the color bar as a direct threat to their livelihoods—which, of course, it is. Some of them do take a longer view and would like to reach an understanding with the African unions now while there is time for a reasonable transition —but I am afraid they're a minority.

"Our long-run problem is simply this: we have a vast, profitable, and promising investment in Africa. Over the years we cannot develop that investment without the friendly coöperation of the Africans. The Rhodesias are no longer isolated from the world. The Africans here are demanding broader opportunities and we will meet their reasonable demands or eventually be pushed out."

MOST EDUCATED AFRICANS IN THE CENTRAL AFRICAN Federation still hope that a political and economic balance can be worked out between the races. An African dentist in Southern Rhodesia complained bitterly of the discriminations to which his people are subject, but then hastily added:

"Please don't misunderstand me. Not many of us would want to see the Europeans leave Africa. Without their technical and management skills and their development capital, progress would be even slower. But why can't the Europeans in Africa recognize that *they* need *us*, too?

"The place to start is in simple practical coöperation to end racism in our own communities. A while ago I joined with African and European friends here in Salisbury in organizing the Capri-

17

corn Society. Our purpose is to get rid of the color bar in all its manifestations. In Nyasaland they've formed a similar organization—the Interracial Association—with white, Negro, and Asian members.

"We want to develop an *African* way of life where there's room for all races, nationalities, and religions on an equal footing. Who knows—perhaps the Europeans among us may some day accept an African prime minister of the Central Federation as naturally as the Romans accepted their dark-skinned African emperors.

"I studied dentistry in America and I know the stubborn racial problems that you still have left. Yet in industry and in the armed forces able Negroes are now in positions of authority over white Americans. In fact, it's the principle of equality of opportunity which we learned largely from America that drives us now to create a free Africa where everyone—European, Asian, and African—can live in dignity and peace."

In the union of south africa we find a member of the British Commonwealth that offers an even more difficult contrast to the tension-free racial relationships and competent assurance of British West Africa. Alan Paton has called the Afrikaners of South Africa "one of the most virile and upward-striving races of the earth." These qualities have helped to make the Union of South Africa economically by far the most advanced country on the continent. They also helped to create what many observers believe to be the world's only literally hopeless crisis in race relations.

Of South Africa's 12,500,000 people, one out of four is white and well over half of these whites are Afrikaners. Although mainly of Dutch descent, they speak Afrikaans, a language they evolved in Africa. The remainder are of British descent and speak English. In addition to 8,500,000 submerged black Africans, there are a million "coloreds" or mulattoes, 360,000 Indians and Pakistanis, and 40,000 Malayans.

The explosiveness of South Africa's internal conflict lies in the racial attitudes of the Afrikaners who have controlled the Union government since 1948. Former Prime Minister Daniel F. Malan has stated bluntly: "There are only two directions in which a choice can be made. Equality, that is, the abolition of all color discrimination, or *apartheid* . . . which will grant all those on both sides of the color line their own free development and encouragement according to their capacity and their level of civilization. Between them there is no middle way."

The inevitable choice of *apartheid* evolved in part from a religious conviction sanctified in the Boer struggle against both the Bantu Africans and the British. How passionately it is supported I learned from the wife of an Afrikaner businessman.

"South Africa belongs to us Afrikaners at least as much as the United States belongs to you Americans. My Dutch ancestors settled in South Africa only a few years after other Dutchmen settled in New York. They treated the native Hottentots no better or no worse than your American ancestors treated the Red Indians.

"The British arrived here much later to set up supply stations on the long sea route to India and China. When missionaries with their foolish talk

19

of brotherhood stirred up trouble among the Africans my Boer forefathers left the coast to trek further up into the interior. There they built their pastoral republics on the basis of 'no equality in Church or State.' The Bantus they met there for the first time were pushing down in a great migration from Central Africa. These black Africans, as anyone can see, have a weaker historical claim to South Africa than American Indians have to the continental United States. They came after we did.

"For many years everything went smoothly. Then the discovery of gold and diamonds brought British fortune hunters who pushed our people aside. A bitter war developed between British and Boers in 1899 which we lost.

"The Union government that took charge was composed of conscience-stricken Britishers, hoodwinked Boers, adventurers and dreamers. It was despised from the beginning by all good Afrikaners. Now we have at last won political control, and we are determined to build the one kind of state in which the white man can survive in Africa.

"We have been waiting for 300 years for this opportunity, and we are not going to be stopped now by moralizers in the United States, the United Kingdom, and the United Nations, or by softer elements in our own country.

"We are Afrikaners, not Britons or Europeans. We have our own language. This is our only country. We have no other place to go. We are not transients or adventurers. We are people of Africa.

20

"*Apartheid* is the one way of preserving and developing our cultural heritage. It is also the one way in which the nonwhites can develop whatever capacities they may have. Generations of Afrikaners have learned this lesson by bitter experience.

"God Himself created the difference in races—we didn't. In the Book of Genesis, Ham, the dark-skinned son of Noah who was sent to populate Africa, is described as a 'servant of servants.' In the Book of Ruth his people are referred to as 'hewers of wood and drawers of water.' In South Africa today, as many leaders of our Dutch Reformed Church have pointed out, we Afrikaners are simply carrying out the will of God."

APARTHEID IS IMPLEMENTED BY A FANTASTIC COMPLEX of segregation regulations that make life almost intolerable for nonwhites and a burden even on the whites it has been designed to "protect." Perhaps the cruelest of these regulations are the pass laws, which make even the most casual movement of any African subject to the whim of any white. Although the framework of these restrictions was laid generations ago, the fanatically racist governments of Dr. Malan and Mr. Strydom have intensified them.

Under the circumstances, it is remarkable to find an African who can approach this subject calmly. Yet many still do. This is what an elderly Negro clergyman in South Africa has to say.

"*Apartheid*, of course, is designed to assure the permanent dominance of the European. The claim that *apartheid* will result in 'free development' on our side of the color line is a piece of deception designed to give these arrogant racists a plausible excuse.

"*Apartheid* can be laughed out of court on a practical basis. The literal application of the principle of *apartheid* would bring about the collapse of our economy. In separate societies the Afrikaners would have no one to work their factories and mines. Yet they know that once they modify their position, reasonable people, regardless of race, will turn toward the very compromise and coöperation which they fear most.

"In this age no state can survive indefinitely that ignores the interests of a majority of its people. The nonwhite races make up 80 per cent of South Africa's population and we will never accept this system. We won't accept it because permanent servility is a denial of the dignity of man.

"No, *apartheid* is nonsense, however you look at it. Father Trevor Huddleston has called it 'blasphemy.' Even some leading members of the Dutch Reformed Church have condemned it. Dr. B. B. Kect, President of the Dutch Reformed Seminary at Stellenbosch, recently called it 'an escape from our Christian duty' and added, 'the Scriptures say that everyone is my neighbor, and if this is so, I must associate with him.'

"Yet there *apartheid* stands like a stone wall. When we put forward our own claims for advancement we are labeled Communist agitators and radicals. A whole legal system has been erected to punish us Africans for furthering our own rights.

"South Africa needs the skills and the capital of the people of European stock. We Africans, Coloreds, and Asians want to coöperate with them, to live and let live. Fifty years ago here in South Africa Gandhi began his first experiments with nonviolent resistance in defense of Indian rights. We have prayed that his philosophy of nonviolence might achieve our emancipation here as it did for the Indians in India.

"But now we realize that nonviolence succeeded because the British had a conscience which put some limit on their suppression. In Gandhi's day the government here in South Africa was headed by General Smuts who also had a conscience, so progress was made. But how can nonviolence succeed here now against this government of fanatics?

"Like many other South Africans, I have given my life to this struggle against injustice. I shall never regret the effort. But now the gulf between the races is widening, my people are going backward, and the explosion is only a question of time.

"Not until Dr. Malan came to power was a Communist elected to the South African Parliament. When he was ejected, another was elected in his place, and then still another. The Suppression of Communism Act has been used ruthlessly. Yet there are now far more Communists here than in all the rest of Africa south of the Sahara.

"As my generation of moderates fails, dies, and is forgotten, the leadership will pass to them. Eager young Communists will rally our people, match fanaticism with fanaticism, and some day plunge South Africa into a blood bath that will wash not only over Africa, but perhaps the world. I can see no other outcome."

In the africa of france, belgium, and portugal, we find sharply different views and objectives. France has no possession in Africa that she calls a colony. Algeria is presumed to be part of metropolitan France. Then there are "overseas territories" which are now part of the "French Union" and presumably, according to the French plan, on their way to becoming part of France— French West Africa, French Equatorial Africa, French Somaliland, Madagascar.

In addition, there are Morocco and Tunisia, which are rapidly moving toward self-government under French general direction, and the French-administered United Nations trust territories of Togoland and the Camerouns. All together, as we have seen, the French flag flies over more than one-third of Africa, an area substantially larger than the United States. Yet France's 50,000,000 African subjects include only 1,500,000 Frenchmen, most of whom are farmers living in North Africa.

Although the French government is rapidly withdrawing its authority in Tunisia and Morocco and the French position has become steadily weaker in Algeria, most of these French settlers remain uncompromising on the subject of North African independence. Here is one typical view from Algeria:

"Foreign meddlers should stop urging us to carry out policies we have no intention of carrying out. Why do you assume without question that self-government is the best course? We deny it flatly. Those who praised us for agreeing to autonomy in Morocco and Tunisia are mistaken. Those were not reforms. They were backward steps to which a weak government in Paris agreed under pressure.

"We regard the Africans in our overseas territories as Frenchmen or Frenchmen-to-be. In our dealings with them we have no racial consciousness such as you have in America and the British have in East Africa, and we erect no racial barriers. This means that every African in French territory can enjoy all the benefits of French civilization. Our ideal has always been assimilation.

"Today, 52 of the 626 seats in our National Assembly in Paris are held by Africans; in the Council of the Republic there are 38 Africans out of the total of 320. Their privileges and duties are the same as those of the other deputies and senators. They are full citizens of France.

"Thus the African can share equally in all cultural and economic advantages of our French world society. Why should he give up these certain benefits for the mirage of an independence which in reality would only mean his ruination?"

EVEN LESS TOLERANT OF OUTSIDE OPINION IS THE TYPICAL high-ranking French military official in North Africa. He lives in the long shadow cast by the illustrious Marshal Lyautey, the builder of modern Morocco. But he is more likely these days to reflect Lyautey's cantankerousness than his constructive achievements.

"The proposition is an extremely simple one. Are we not all part of the Atlantic alliance? Isn't strict French control of North Africa essential to the effectiveness of NATO? Without us, what would become of Allied control of the Mediterranean? Can we depend on the Arabs to contain the Soviet Union? The creation of a Eurafrican bloc is the key to the West's security. We French were pushed out of Syria and Lebanon by British and American pressure—and what a mess the Middle East is in today.

"The difficulties we now face in North Africa started in 1943 when President Roosevelt stopped in Casablanca and encouraged the Sultan to seek independence. From that moment Sidi Mohammed ben Youssef was no longer reliable. Today any North African extremist who attacks us can find support somewhere in America.

"Our nation is bedeviled from within and without by pacifists, pro-Africans, misguided humanitarians, and liberals who prattle about freedom, but who have never had to face the hard realities of administration here in Africa. France, itself, can absorb the chaos of French politics. But indecision in the face of outside pressure is fatal to an empire. It has already cost us dearly in Asia. We who love France are determined to preserve what's left of her glory here in Africa."

ARAB AND BERBER NATIONALISTS, AS MIGHT BE EXPECTED, have a different view about the destiny of France in North Africa. Today they speak with the assurance of those who know that the future is on their side.

"Isn't it tragic to see the French struggling so in this web of their own making? Why do they refuse to learn from their failure in Indochina? They seem to be possessed by a suicide impulse. If you Americans continue to support them here in Algeria, your position in Asia as well as throughout Africa will grow worse.

26

"We don't want to see France ruined and we don't want Frenchmen to leave our countries. The French in many ways are an inspired people who have made some magnificent contributions to Africa. They can stay and coöperate in the new national society. We want them and need them, but not on their terms.

"The French are still trying to pretend that they are a great imperial power. They dream of somehow recapturing the glory of the grand monarch Louis XIV or even Napoleon. Why can't they see that France ceased to be a great power after the terrible sacrifices she made in World War I? Why can't the French face this hard fact with dignity, and live in peace with those who want to be their friends?

"Their insistence that because we live under the French flag we are Frenchmen fools nobody—not even themselves. We are Algerians. We are Moroccans. We are Tunisians. We are Muslims. We are Africans. Our cultures are older than that of the French and we have no intention of giving them up.

"If the 8,000,000 Algerians are *really* Frenchmen, should not the French government hang its head in shame? Most of us so-called 'Frenchmen' are as miserable as the peasants of Iraq or Iran—illiterate, half-starved, and burdened with disease. Our income averages only $80 a year—one-tenth that of the French. When we protest, they say: 'Give us time. You mustn't expect improvements overnight.' But how much time do our French friends want? They have been governing Algeria now for 125 years.

"We have watched other Muslims win independence throughout Asia and Africa—in Indonesia, Pakistan, Syria, Lebanon, Saudi Arabia, Egypt, Jordan, Iraq, Yemen, the Sudan, and now right next to us in Libya. Does anybody believe we are less ready for independence than Libya? And what about Tunisia where Habib Bourguiba has been proving the North African's capacity for responsible, democratic self-government?

"There is still time for the French to reach a civilized accord with us. They will reach it with us soon; or ultimately they will yield to the extremists as they were forced to yield in Indochina."

THE PORTUGUESE, LIKE THE FRENCH, ARE ALSO COMmitted to "assimilating" the African, and they have established complex official machinery for this purpose. Any African who meets certain educational, religious, financial, and social standards may become an *assimilado* and the equal of any other Portuguese citizen. Since the Portuguese control these standards, the *assimilados* are kept in a manageable minority and find themselves set apart from other Africans. In Angola, Mozambique, and Portuguese Guinea, with a combined population of some 10,000,000 Africans, less than one-half of one per cent are *assimilados*.

The Portuguese were the first Europeans to come to Africa in modern times and they confidently assert they will be the last to leave. Although government advisory councils recently have been set up with carefully screened African representatives, Portuguese Africa is among the most backward areas in the world and, at the moment, as

28

insulated as any area in this modern age could be against the blasts of nationalism. Consequently, most Portuguese officials still appear relaxed and confident. Here is a typical view:

"Our Prince Henry the Navigator, our Bartholomeu Diaz and Vasco da Gama explored the African coast before Columbus crossed the Atlantic. Since then we have had one unswerving objective here: to convert the Blacks to the only true faith, to lift them from their moral and material misery, to clothe them and house them to the greatest practical extent, to instruct them in the basic essentials of civilization, and to receive in return a just reward for our efforts.

"Misinformed outsiders who denounce our program are hurting the unfortunate people whom they profess to want to help. Anyone who honestly accepts the achievements of our Christian way of life, which is the very basis of civilization, must agree that we have a moral duty to spread these achievements.

"Those who take the contrary view are in effect arguing that primitive society should remain in darkness, that cruelty, ignorance, and fear should be perpetuated, and that millions of human beings should be abandoned to the witch doctors and head hunters.

"Today the greatest enemy of religious law is communism. There is no question of where Portugal stands in the face of this challenge. We shall continue to hold our own, here and at home. In one way Russia has done us a service: its propagandists have made the words 'imperialism' and

'colonialism' synonomous with the foreign policy
of any non-Communist state. Thus these words
have become quite meaningless."

THE CONGO IS IN MANY WAYS A REFRESHING PLACE. THE
Belgians make no bones about it. Theirs is a colony ruled
by Belgians—by Belgians from *Belgium.* There are no
political parties in the Congo because none are allowed.
Nobody votes, not even the Belgians who live there, which,
the Belgians point out, proves the absence of racial discrimination.

The objective of a prosperous industrial Congo is being pursued relentlessly. Although the task of prospecting
for mineral wealth has scarcely been begun, the Congo
already produces half the world's uranium, 80 per cent
of the world's cobalt and industrial diamonds, and 10
per cent of the world's copper and tin. The Congo River
and its tributaries are an inexhaustible source of hydro-
electric power.

In developing this rich area, the Belgians have not
neglected the Congolese. Economic progress is impressive and, in the cities at least, it is broadly shared. Belgian officials feel an understandable pride in their accomplishments:

"In less than fifty years, we have brought peace
where there was formerly continuous tribal war-
fare. We have stamped out cannibalism. We have
introduced Christianity where there was formerly
only paganism. We have established French as
a common language, and created one of the two
most literate colonies in Africa. We have built
hospitals and public-health clinics.

30

"Above all, we have revealed the unlimited future of the Congo to the Congolese. Today there are steadily expanding opportunities for many of the 12,000,000 Congolese to earn high wages and to enjoy the highest standard of living in African history. Already the average Congolese textile worker gets $2 a day in addition to a house, food allowance, and medical care. Congolese schoolteachers receive wages only slightly less than your Negro teachers in Mississippi.

"Political rights of the natives will come more slowly. We have our own *evolué* system. As rapidly as the individual Congolese proves his stability and capacity to carry responsibility, he is given full citizenship rights to go with those responsibilities.

"To give illiterate and backward Africans the right to vote is madness. Nor does it make sense to send hundreds of Africans to study abroad as the British do with the predictable result that they will come home restless, unhappy and full of radical ideas.

"Our first job is to train the African to earn his own living in the modern industrial world. This means basic education and technical training. Once a healthy economic base has been established, there can be the gradual development of higher education and political responsibility.

"In the meantime, we will not repeat the mistake that the British made in East Africa, and the French in North Africa. We will allow no Belgian settlers to come to the Congo to steal the African's land."

31

ETHIOPIA, LIBYA, LIBERIA, EGYPT, SUDAN, AND SOUTH
Africa are the only self-governing nations of Africa—
although, as we have seen, the Gold Coast, Nigeria,
Tunisia, and Morocco may join them soon. Apart from
the brief Italian occupation before the war, Ethiopia,
indeed, has been independent for 3,000 years. Its dominant Amhara, who speak one of Africa's few written
languages, consider themselves Semites. Their religion
is Orthodox of the same strain as the Coptic Christian
Church of Egypt.

Ethiopia's poverty and political backwardness are
abysmal. Indeed with the exception of Nepal, this is the
most isolated and primitive country I have ever visited.
Yet here, as elsewhere in Africa, there is a vigorous
drive for economic and political progress. Emperor
Haile Selassie, the King of Kings, is striving to intro-
duce democratic techniques and to lay the groundwork
for a constitutional democracy.

Ethiopia is also world-minded. An army officer who
served in the Ethiopian contingent in Korea explains
why this is so.

"I shall always remember our emperor's
speech to us when we departed as soldiers of the
United Nations for service halfway around the
world. The emperor reminded us that Ethiopia
was the first victim of World War II. He said that
our country must make all necessary sacrifices to
help avoid World War III, and he urged us to
fight bravely to defend South Korea from Communist aggression.

"You will find many foreigners here in Ethiopia. The two principal advisers in our Foreign
Office are Americans. There are many more
able Americans here in your Point Four Program.

In addition, we have Swiss to help organize our finances, and Canadians to help set up our educational system. Our army has Swedish advisers and our police is being organized by British experts. Our best hospital is run by doctors and nurses from the Soviet Union whose predecessors were sent here in 1912 by Czar Nicholas II who also had ambitions in this part of the world.

"We welcome foreign help, but we are jealous of our independence and we have no intention of losing it. We shall also remain faithful to our ancient national traditions. We have little in common, as you know, with the rest of Africa, and nothing at all with the Bantu Africans."

Nevertheless in the trusteeship territories of British Tanganyika, Italian Somaliland, Belgian Ruanda-Urundi, French and British Cameroons, French and British Togoland, and South-West Africa under the Union of South Africa, we find many Africans who are disillusioned with the postwar promise of the United Nations. An African leader in Tanganyika expresses his views in the following terms:

"First the League of Nations and then the United Nations accepted responsibility for our future, and each has disappointed us. These mandates or trust territories could have been a democratic proving ground where Europeans and Africans together might demonstrate that orderly progress towards self-government is possible in Africa as elsewhere. But because the United Nations has been dominated by the Atlantic bloc, we remain little more than colonial appendages.

"Look at South-West Africa. It was given to South Africa as a mandate by the League of Nations and its transfer to the jurisdiction of the Trusteeship Council was projected by the United Nations Charter. What is it now? No more and no less than a colonial possession of the most racist government the world has ever seen, and I include Nazi Germany. The majority in the United Nations with all its talk of democracy and freedom couldn't muster its courage to stop it.

"And take my own Tanganyika. In January, 1955, a committee of the Trusteeship Council finally agreed to propose a timetable to *suggest* to the British administering power our step-by-step progress toward self-government in twenty to twenty-five years. We were so happy when the American delegates voted for this proposal, for we felt that American policy makers were at last coming to grips with African realities.

"But the British protested, the State Department beat a retreat, and the American delegate was instructed to reverse his position at the next Trusteeship meeting. Both Thomas Jefferson and Abraham Lincoln must have turned over in their graves."

IN ASIA CHRISTIAN MISSIONARIES HAVE BEEN COMPETING with deeply rooted religions even older than their own. In non-Muslim Africa, most of the people were pagans whose religious life was dominated by witch doctors. Perhaps this is why European and American missionaries in Africa have won more Christian converts than in all of Asia combined. The total is thought to be 21,000,000.

Yet the Christian influence has been cut from many different pieces of cloth. A European missionary with his feet still firmly planted in the nineteenth century and his shoulders heavy with the "white man's burden" offers this traditional view of his role in Africa:

"The hardship and sacrifice that have gone into our African missions must eventually yield great results. We draw strength from the misery around us, and a greater faith in the future.

"Many people ask when the Africans will outgrow our tutelage. My answer to this question is simple: the Africans will never be capable of self-government. We who have had experience here see the African as he is, and we know that for him self-government would be a profound mistake.

"Sentimentalists in America and Europe believe that political freedom and individualism are universally applicable. Yet it is not true that mankind has always advanced best under these circumstances.

"It is no accident that the African has never learned to make a large basket. He is too lazy to carry one. Moreover, when someone steals his small basket, his loss is small. Frankly, these people are children and will always be so. It is our Christian duty, as elder brothers, to care for them."

A NEW DEDICATED GENERATION OF CHRISTIAN MISSIONaries takes sharp issue with such race-conscious paternalism. Here is a hearteningly typical view:

"Christianity is the dynamic force that has awakened Africa. So far the Bible has had far more impact here than the ideas of Karl Marx. It was the Christian missionary who introduced the Western-type education which has taught Africans that all men are entitled to equal rights, opportunities, and responsibilities.

"What this means in day-to-day terms has been shown them in many ways including self-help efforts in the villages to improve health and agriculture. For these gains, our Christian churches, both Protestant and Catholic, have been largely responsible, and I am profoundly proud that this is so.

"Our Christian movement in Africa still lacks properly trained missionary leaders and we suffer from senseless sectarian divisions. Yet I believe our greatests barrier to faster progress is the behavior of the white man himself. Most Europeans in Africa describe themselves as Christians, and south of the Sahara, Africans *assume* that all white men are Christians.

"This means that Christianity itself, for better of for worse, has become totally identified with the conduct of the European in Africa. When his conduct fails to reflect the Christian ideal of human brotherhood, our entire cause suffers. Many Africans see the way Christ's teachings have been distorted by Europeans who call themselves Christians. So they feel free to distort them in their own way. Thus we should not be surprised to hear that last November in Kenya in the knapsack of a dead Mau Mau general they found a Bible.

"In some cases the insistence of the 'old Africa hands' that Africans are incapable of self-government may be an honest rationalization, but more often it is a devious device to help Europeans keep control. Yet how can men still say these things when such Africans as Nkrumah and Gbedemah in the Gold Coast and Azikiwe in Nigeria have been proving them ridiculous?

"As I see it, the American missionary in Africa has a special responsibility. As an *American* he must never forget that it was the political idealism of Jefferson, Lincoln, Wilson, and Roosevelt that inspired African nationalism. If we deny the validity of these ideals now for the people of other races and creeds here in Africa, we shall stand self-condemned as hypocrites and imposters.

"As a *Christian* he must remember that even the highest secular ideals are not a substitute for Christ's message of love. Racial tensions in Africa are no longer susceptible to a purely political approach. Only the overwhelming force of God's love can effectively reach hearts and minds twisted with fear and racial bitterness."

STILL ANOTHER MISSIONARY APPROACHES AFRICA FROM a less familiar perspective. He is the modern manifestation of the age-old Arab drive into the great African continent that started thirteen centuries ago. His skin is dark and he moves easily among the Africans, sleeping in their huts, eating their food, living their customs. This is what he says:

"My name is Abdul Hamid, and I am a Muslim missionary, a graduate of Al Azhar University in Cairo which has been the chief center of Islamic learning for the past 1,000 years. In Mecca in August, 1955, the premiers of Egypt and Pakistan and the king of Saudi Arabia determined that Islam should be carried to every corner of the continent. This means that my new work will take me deep into Africa; I will be followed soon by many other Muslim missionaries.

"Mediterranean Africa has long been loyal to Islam. We have many adherents in East Africa and Nigeria. Our 60,000,000 African Muslims already outnumber African Christians three to one.

"All of Africa must now become our special concern, for the African people can no longer be left without a revealed religion. Let me speak bluntly. The Christian missionaries are failing because they disrupt Africa's pattern of life and then put nothing enduring in its place. Consciously or not, Christianity maintains the subservience of the Africans and plays into the hands of those Europeans who would like to dominate and exploit Africa indefinitely. With its strict social order Islam gives Africans a greater sense of security. It is the one alternative faith that can save the Africans from paganism and at the same time encourage their independent political and economic development.

"But I hope that Europeans will realize that our long-term efforts here will be helpful to them. As Premier Nasser has said, 'The establishment of Islam in Africa will be a firm shield against communism.' "

In the face of these many conflicting outside pressures the majority of Africans still reject all foreign concepts—religious, economic, or political. The old ways of Africa stubbornly maintain their influence, and their earnest and effective defenders include thousands of tribal chiefs and subchiefs. These comments by a chief in the central Gold Coast express a deeply held view which you will hear in most parts of Africa:

"The tribal way of life is still the only stable foundation of African society. My people are like children. They really understand only our own customs. Without them they would be lost.

"Many Europeans have been wise enough to respect and preserve these tribal ways and we are grateful to them. Yet more and more we see young Africans spend a few years at Oxford or Harvard and return full of half-digested ideas about freedom and democracy, to stir up our people against the proven ways of their forefathers. That's why many of us older Africans are in no hurry to see the Europeans abandon their authority here."

To these earnest African voices I might add many others, each offering its own variation on this complex theme. But these should be enough to demonstrate that modern Africa is both contradictory and vigorous in expressing its hopes, fears, and prejudices.

39

When we examine these views more carefully, we find that a number of patterns begin to emerge that help to remove some of Africa's mystery. In the next chapter I shall seek to unravel the more important threads and to isolate, if I can, the common denominators with which American policy makers must come to grips.

II

The Scope of the Challenge

The history of the next twenty years may largely be written around the interplay of three forces which already profoundly influence world politics. When we examine the widely contradictory viewpoints which we encountered in the first chapter against the background of these forces, the problems and conflicts of Africa take on new meaning and even some sense of order.

The first of these has been described as the Revolution of Rising Expectations. This revolution, which shapes the attitudes and aspirations of the one and a half billion people of India, Africa, and South America, has three objectives: freedom from foreign domination, political or economic; a full measure of human dignity regardless of race, religion or color; and increased economic opportunities, broadly shared.

The second of these forces, and most often overlooked, is the pace at which the Atlantic nations including the United States are devouring their indigenous raw materials and becoming dependent on imports from the underdeveloped continents of Asia, Africa, and South America. Although this situation is not yet urgent, it has explosive implications for the long haul. We may recall that the shortage of raw materials in Germany and Japan was one of the factors leading to World War II.

The third force is the political, economic, military, and ideological competition between the Atlantic nations and their associates led by the United States, on the one hand, and the Communist nations led by the Soviet Union, on the other.

The interplay of these forces inevitably creates pressures and conflicts even between nations whose long-term interests are similar if not identical. In the past few years, for instance, the Atlantic nations have given highest priority to measures opposing Communist military and political expansion; the focus of new nations recently emerged from colonial domination or peoples still under such domination has been on the earliest achievement of political and economic freedom and social dignity.

Thus NATO leaders, basing their arguments on what they believed to be the imminent danger of a shooting war, have insisted that they cannot at this stage consider the issue of colonialism on its merits; while most leaders of dependent or recently dependent nations, sharply discounting the possibility of armed Soviet aggression, have argued that international communism is less of a danger to their interest than the military defense maneuvers of those who seek to contain it.

Now let us examine each of these three forces separately in its relation to the political and economic future of this vast and promising continent.

I. THE REVOLUTION OF RISING EXPECTATIONS

The End of Colonialism

We have seen that the first objective of the Revolution of Rising Expectations is self-determination, and that Africa is the last major stronghold of European colonialism. The only independent African nations are Ethiopia, Egypt, Liberia, the Union of South Africa, Libya, and the Sudan. Add Tunisia, Morocco, and the Gold Coast which may become free by 1957, and Somaliland and perhaps Nigeria by 1960, and still only a little more than half of Africa's 200,000,000 people will be free.

When an observer seeks to describe the strong currents of disaffection which are shaking colonial Africa, he instinctively finds himself thinking in traditional terms of nationalism. Yet in Africa the word itself must be used cautiously.

In its broadest sense, "nationalist" may be used to describe an immensely wide variety of disaffected groups throughout Africa. Some of them have their base in a regional alignment created originally by the colonial power, as in the Gold Coast. Others stem from the older tribal structure of native society, as in Nigeria. Still others have their roots in a radical messianic movement under the fanatic leadership of a native figure, such as the earlier Mahdist movement in the Sudan and the Mau Mau in Kenya.

These diversified roots of Africa nationalism result

in a situation which varies from area to area. But to the extent that such disaffected groups can be termed nationalist in aim—that is to the extent that their focus is political independence—they seem to share one common objective throughout the continent: the early creation of institutions identical with those of the colonizing country whether or not they fit the local situation. This may be merely a transitional phase. But it makes for a powerful force.

It would be inaccurate to say that the objective of self-determination is now vigorously sought or even understood by more than a large minority of the 100,-000,000 Africans who have no immediate prospect of independence. But it would be folly to assume that the widespread indifference that still exists will continue to defy the efforts of African leaders to prod it into action. Inevitably, the powerful and growing force of nationalism will soon reach into the most remote villages of the continent.

For some time the Arab and Berber Muslims of North Africa have had well-developed independence movements influenced by the successful nationalism of Egypt and the Middle East. The self-government experiments in British West Africa will be carefully watched by all of Bantu Africa. The independence movement in Africa has also drawn inspiration from America's revolutionary break with British colonialism, from the words of our Declaration of Independence, and from the historic stand taken by such Americans as Lincoln, Wilson, and Roosevelt in favor of the self-determination of peoples.

Yet African nationalism is most immediately influenced by the independence movements in Asia since the war, and particularly in India. Africans are increasingly subject to the same internal impulses, external influences and inexorable historic processes that have already redrawn the maps of Asia. The success of Asian nationalism in achieving independence for some 600,000,000 people in eight years convinced African leaders that they are part of a mighty world movement and gave them new confidence to press their own demands.

In a sense Africa's revolutionary objectives were formalized at the Bandung conference in April, 1955. Although the African representatives were few in number they made it clear that the aspirations of this great continent were not subject to major compromise, and the new leaders of Asia, including the prime minister of the People's Republic of China, committed thᵊmselves to support these aspirations.

This conference of 28 nations, representing five-eighths of all the people of the world, would have been an event of historic importance under any circumstances. But its impact was heightened by the curious mixture of self-deception, nervousness, and arrogance with which it was viewed from the capitals of the Atlantic powers. One Washington official went so far as to sum up the State Department's attitude as one of "benevolent indifference." Nothing could illustrate more vividly the failure of many Western leaders to grasp the political significance of what is happening in Africa and Asia.

The African voices which in the previous chapter demanded self-government and a full measure of human dignity and opportunity simply cannot be ignored. Whether they are "right" or "wrong" from one point of view or another, or something in between, is beside the point. They are authentic. They mean what they say.

In terms of institutions, experience, and civil servants most of Africa at this stage is less well equipped for self-rule than the Asians were after the war; Africans also have less faith than the Asians had in the effectiveness of the United Nations and in the sincerity of the Atlantic nations, including the United States. But such factors only add new and explosive dimensions to the classic colonial situation. And there are many others.

Much of Africa, for instance, is not far removed from what it was before the Europeans came. To create viable nations out of a people whose sense of loyalty is still limited to tribe, family, or clan, is obviously difficult. It is equally difficult to satisfy demands for self-determination and a full measure of human dignity when both concepts may have such differing implications to different peoples.

As soon as the first autonomous cabinet took office in Tunisia, for instance, some Tunisians at once stopped paying street-car fares; others were surprised and outraged when the tax collector appeared on schedule. To these emancipated Tunisians, self-determination was a totally personal concept.

The diversity of life, culture, and language creates similar barriers to cohesive agreement on objectives. There are some 800 African tribes and languages as well as thousands of dialects. In Tanganyika, the Congo, and other regions, there are many tribes that communicate with each other with great difficulty or not at all.

Nor are the difficulties in communication confined to language differences or even to illiteracy which probably averages 85 per cent, with the lowest level in the Gold Coast, Uganda, and the Congo and the highest in the Portuguese colonies. As we have seen, tribal chiefs in the bush sometimes mistrust the detribalized African intellectuals of the cities rather more than they do the Europeans who control their central governments.

Very real difficulties also arise from the African's lack of political, parliamentary, and administrative experience. Equally great are the problems that grow out of the rudimentary state of much of the African economy. Without vastly increased production, revenues will continue to be unavailable for adequate education, housing, public health, and communications.

These many obstacles to successful self-government in Africa are formidable, and most educated Africans are keenly aware of this fact. Yet, because the pressures are so great, this knowledge will not materially slow down their demand for freedom. Colonial authorities, no matter how sincere, who use these difficulties to continue their tight economic and political control only fan the growing unrest and make whatever hope there may be for the orderly evolution of self-government that much less.

This is particularly so because in Africa, as in prewar Asia, the governing groups are of one race, the governed of another. The mixture is inevitably explosive, and it brings us to the second objective of the Revolution of Rising Expectations—human dignity regardless of race or color.

Racial Equality

The most extreme racial discrimination exists, of course, in the white self-governing Union of South Africa. But, colonial government policy statements to the contrary, a European-imposed color bar exists to some extent in most of *colonial* Africa, varying in degree from its highest level of restrictiveness in Kenya and Southern Rhodesia to its lowest in the Portuguese colonies, British West Africa, French West Africa and French Equatorial Africa. This barrier affects and often embitters every aspect of economic and political life, and, in greater or lesser degrees, dominates all relationships between Europeans and Africans.

In its extreme form, as we find it in *apartheid*, it is based on the assumption, explicit and implicit, that any white man is superior to any nonwhite, and that indeed God planned it that way. In its most moderate phase, the white man is cast in the role of a kind of elder brother who, because of his superior status in the world, is best fitted to make the principal decisions. This latter view is expressed by European leaders who expand Cecil Rhodes' widely quoted concept, "equal rights for all civilized men," to include equal rights for all to become civilized.

The African's resentment against current racial indignities is intensified by his long experience with the white man which extends back to the brutalities of slave-trading days and the nineteenth-century era of colonial conquest.

Most educated Africans are no less aware than the Europeans of the primitive conditions in which most of Africa still lives. But as I have pointed out, they resent what they believe to be the white man's use of this circumstance as an excuse to continue and even strengthen his political and economic control.

These racial elements give African nationalism a quality of almost frightening intensity and of corresponding urgency. They evoke a force far more basic than a desire for recognition of political and economic rights —the primal urge to be recognized in the first instance as human beings worthy and capable of appreciating human rights. We have seen that this urge arises from the depths of the African's soul and it will accept no ultimate compromise.

48

Thus the drive toward racial emancipation not only parallels and propels political nationalism in Africa, but often transcends it. Indeed, South Africa, where the drive is strongest, is an independent country where political nationalism is not an issue. To colonial Africa, the struggle against varying degrees of racial discrimination is in many ways the heart of the colonial question.

The Mau Mau revolt illustrates the terrible potential power of raw racial resentment when it becomes frustrated by the failure of evolutionary change. Although the British regime in Kenya is not the best of African colonial governments, neither is it the worst. The Kikuyu are the most numerous and most advanced of the Kenya tribes.

Yet the development of the Mau Mau conspiracy among the Kikuyu was scarcely suspected until it had burst forth in all its primitive savagery. That such a gulf could develop between the races in a country where the white man has lived side by side with the African for seventy-five years is disheartening.

Certainly the Europeans cannot complain that someone should have warned them. Writing in 1899 of South Africa, Lord Bryce said:

> "Anxieties must press upon the mind of anyone who looks sixty or eighty years forward.
> . . . Whatever those difficulties may be, they will be less formidable if the whites realize, before the native Africans have begun to feel aggrieved, that they have got to live with them, and that the true interests of both races are in the long run the same."

We must hope that Gandhi was wrong when he remarked that the "white man's pride of race" may prove incurable.

Economic Well-being

When we consider the third objective of Africa's revolution—rapid economic growth and opportunity—we find that an inherently difficult problem is again gravely compounded by this question of race.

It is virtually impossible to find statistics to describe over-all African living standards. Probably as many as 90 per cent of all Africans live on the land. For most of these people, "income" as conventional economists think of it is virtually non-existent.

The handful of Bantu Africans who are allowed to do skilled or semiskilled work may achieve a moderately comfortable living in the Congo, the Northern Rhodesia mines, or the Gold Coast. However, the number of skilled Bantu workers in Africa is still small. The great majority of Africans who labor in the towns and cities live in poverty.

To them, and to their far more numerous cousins who live a precarious existence on the land, the political-economic equation becomes a simple one; the white man rules, the black man obeys. Therefore, the white man is rich while the black man is poor. A more ominous revolutionary situation is difficult to imagine.

The recurrent impression I received in Africa was of a continent relatively empty of people and yet with great economic promise. This is a particularly striking contrast to Asia.

The Belgian Congo, for example, may prove to be as rich in natural resources as India and its land area is nearly as large. Its population of 12,000,000 is a small fraction of India's 360,000,000.

This circumstance in itself has far-reaching implications for Africa's economic future. In Asia, where so many people clamor for a bare existence, even advanced and courageous governments hesitate to encourage the rapid installation of modern machinery. As a result, wages and purchasing power rise with painful slowness.

In Africa, the relative scarcity of people puts a premium on the use of labor-saving devices. Eventually this should result in higher productivity per worker, increased wages and raised living standards. It should also mean a more mechanized agriculture and a correspondingly easier and more prosperous life on the land.

Yet there are two basic problems that now hinder rapid increase of agricultural production. First, the large amounts of arid land which can be made fertile only through irrigation; and second, the problems growing out of the ownership of the land and its proper cultivation. These complex obstacles will have to be faced frankly and intelligently if mechanization and increased production are to be brought about very rapidly.

While the people of Africa are at the moment among the poorest and most primitive in the world, their continent may turn out to be the richest in those natural resources that make our modern industrial age possible. Vast areas of Africa remain unsurveyed, and most of the natural resources that are known to exist there have not been fully assessed. Yet the natural wealth already coming out of Africa serves as a preview of its stupendous possibilities.

Although few laymen know precisely how much uranium Africa is now producing, it is common knowledge that much of the uranium used to produce our stockpile of nuclear weapons comes from the Congo, and that South Africa has also begun to produce the vital element.

In 1952, Africa produced virtually the entire world's

supply of industrial diamonds. It also produced 94 per cent of the world's columbite and 84 per cent of its cobalt, both indispensable for making the heat-resistant steels used in jet planes; also 41 per cent of its beryllium; 33 per cent of its manganese; 29 per cent of its chrome; 21 per cent of its copper; 13 per cent of its tin. Africa, ironically enough, also produced half the world's supply of gold. Its vast resources of iron ore, manganese and bauxite have been scarcely tapped.

In the *present* economic life of that continent land is the essential resource. It provides not only food for the African people, but also such cash crops as palm oil, sisal, cocoa, peanuts, and coffee for export. Who holds the land, how it is held, and how it is worked—these questions will continue for some time to determine the personal economics of most Africans and, to a larger extent, their politics.

Yet the natural resources which lie under the soil are the capital resources which will help to determine the rate of Africa's economic growth. The distribution of the fruits of this growth will have widespread political repercussions.

Thus in Africa as in Asia, the three dynamic components in the Revolution of Rising Expectations—political freedom, human dignity, and increasing economic opportunities—are closely interlocked. Each feeds the other. Together they add up to a force that will not be denied.

II. AFRICA'S RAW MATERIALS

Under what some still call normal circumstances (by which they mean under the circumstances prevailing in the world up to ten years ago) America would have had a heavy stake in the outcome of this three-pronged revolution.

During the past twenty years the United States industrial machine has consumed more raw materials than in all of our previous existence. Already we are importing half of all our industrial raw material requirements.

By 1970 our present consumption will have doubled, our own resources will have further diminished, and we will be competing with other nations now in the process of rapid industrial growth. If we should be denied access to the raw materials of Asia, we would be seriously handicapped, but we could still maintain our economic growth. But if we were also cut off from the apparently limitless mineral reservoir of Africa, we would face formidable difficulties within a decade even though the resources of Canada and of South America remained available to us.

The very suggestion that the day may come when the Atlantic nations may no longer take what they need from the natural resources of Asia and Africa will be dismissed by many as preposterous. Since the fifteenth century the naval power of Britain, Holland, France, Portugal, Spain, and later the United States, singly or in combination, has controlled the seas and therefore controlled the world's primary wealth.

Many American and Western European policy makers still seem to assume that this state of affairs is part of the ultimate pattern of life, and quite beyond the reach of earthly forces. In an age in which traditional political, economic, and technological concepts are being turned upside down, this assumption, so long basic to our economic and political growth and influence, deserves careful scrutiny.

We may start this scrutiny with a fact that few thoughtful observers will question: the colonial system which for 200 years or more has provided the principal machinery of raw material control, is almost certainly in its final stages. In a single decade London has lost the power finally to decide when, on what terms, and for whose benefit the natural wealth of India, Pakistan, Burma, or Ceylon will be used. The Dutch in the Hague and the French in Paris no longer control the wealth of Indonesia and Indochina. The Middle East, which contains 80 per cent of the oil reserves of the entire non-Communist world, has thrown off the last vestiges of Western political domination.

Thus the ability of the heavily industrialized Atlantic powers to command the resources of Asia and the Middle East as well as South America is now largely determined, not by political or military ties, but by *mutual* economic self-interest. It is only a question of time before this will also be true in Africa. As the political grip of the colonial powers becomes weaker, the disposal of Africa's vast wealth will be increasingly decided by Africans.

Under normal, peaceful conditions there is no reason to doubt that this revolutionary development would be in the long-term interest of everyone concerned—much as it might disturb the habits and complacency of the old Asia and Africa hands. As the era of colonial exploitation draws to a close, we could expect a new emphasis on improved living standards which would create expanding overseas markets for both domestic and imported goods.

In spite of their past indifference to local interests and sensibilities, the Atlantic nations have had long and close associations with Asia and Africa. Most Asian and African leaders attended European and American universities, and their philosophy of government is by and large rooted in democratic concepts. The advanced industrial development and ample capital of the Western powers puts them in the best position to supply the goods which the underdeveloped nations need for their own growth. For all of these reasons we might assume a mutually profitable economic association for many generations.

Yet, for two reasons, the permanence of this essential economic and political association can no longer be taken for granted.

First, American policy makers and many of their NATO associates have failed, for the most part, to recognize the emerging new dimensions of power and hence have consistently wasted our natural advantages. Although a lasting partnership between the new nations of Africa and Asia and the Atlantic powers can only be built on a solid foundation of political economic and ideological understanding and self-interest, our policies have remained narrowly focused on the military aspects of the Cold War. And thus the gap between us has steadily widened.

Second, the Soviet Union, keenly aware of the new forces which are moving the underdeveloped nations and with its productive power rapidly expanding, has been working its way into a position from which it can offer an alternative association.

III. The Cold War

This inevitable introduction of Cold War politics and pressures into an area seething with discontent and of profound economic importance to the industrial West, gives this difficult situation a special urgency.

As we saw in the first chapter, the reaction of many colonial spokesmen to the Cold War has been a stiffened determination to maintain the African status quo. Concessions to African nationalism at this time, they argue, would only endanger an increasingly important source of the free world's strategic raw materials and expose African dependencies to Communist political penetration. It is often difficult to know when such fears are sincerely held and when they are being used as an excuse by those who would resist change under any circumstances. In any case, they make a bad situation worse.

It was inevitable that modern Africa's political, economic, and social aspirations would be caught up in the highly charged atmosphere of the Cold War, and that the United Nations would become a forum for discussion and debate. The United Nations Trusteeship System, as we shall see in the final chapter, has provided a permanent and often effective instrument whereby the nationalist leaders of the seven African trust territories can publicize their views. On certain questions, the General Assembly itself has been used to air the grievances of African peoples.

The newly independent nations of Asia and the Middle East, are learning how to make effective use of this United Nations machinery in behalf of areas not yet free; while the Soviet Union, which, in a single decade has brought more formerly independent people under its totalitarian wing than live in all of colonial Africa, has managed skillfully to associate itself with the opponents of the more traditional colonialism.

This in turn has fed the popular American rationalization that all foreign-policy problems originate in Moscow and presumably led Mr. Dulles in his maiden speech as Secretary of State to suggest that the Soviet Union is *creating* the revolutionary unrest which is now keeping so much of Africa in ferment. Thus our fascination with the activities of our adversary has served again to twist our perspective, blind us to the real nature of the forces which are at work, and, most harmful of all, maneuver us into appearing to support the hated and doomed status quo.

The Cold War, as well as sentiment and history, have made the nations of the Atlantic our essential military and political allies. Because these nations control the bulk of Africa we have felt forced to soft-pedal our traditonal anticolonial instincts. In thus approaching Africa through the capitals of the European colonial powers, we have, in the eyes of many Africans, assumed the reactionary coloration of these capitals. And because our support for our NATO allies on colonial questions has been given self-consciously, grudgingly, and with a bad conscience, it has never been wholly satisfactory to them.

THE NEW APPROACH TOWARD THE UNDERDEVELOPED uncommitted world of Asia and Africa on which Khrushchev and his associates embarked in 1955 is a logical development from the grand strategy of world revolution laid down by Lenin more than thirty years ago. Lenin believed that the very existence of democratic capitalism was dependent on colonies and subject nations in Asia and Africa. The ultimate victory of communism, he said, would come through a revolutionary alliance with these exploited peoples.

Soviet dogma held that "The world is divided into two camps . . . the camp of those handful of nations which possess capital and exploit the vast majority of people of the globe . . . and the camp of the majority, the oppressed peoples of the colonies and dependent countries." Communism, it was said, is destined to provide the leadership of the second camp.

On December 29, 1955, before the Supreme Soviet of the U.S.S.R. Khrushchev focussed the concepts of Lenin on present-day Africa:

> "The time when the colonialists could lord it over their dependent peoples is receding into the past. Yet the colonialists . . . do not want to give up voluntarily the system which gives them an opportunity to rob whole nations. . . .

> "Africa . . . is all divided up among European and non-European [*sic*] countries. The chains . . . of colonial slavery strangle the peoples of the colonial and dependent countries and arouse their hatred against the colonialists. The people of these countries are rising ever more resolutely against the colonial regimes. We sympathize with this struggle and wish success to the peoples who are waging it."

The official Soviet text notes that at this point Khrushchev was interrupted by "stormy applause."

The long-term global tactics of Soviet policy now seem apparent: to create within the Communist orbit expanding opportunities for the industrial production of Germany and Japan; to develop and broaden Soviet economic and political associations with India, Southeast Asia, and the oil-rich Middle East; and eventually to offer Africa and even South America an opportunity for rapid economic development within an association of states led by the Soviet Union. If this series of steps is successfully accomplished, America within the next generation may find that it has been isolated—militarily, politically, and economically—from the resources and the people upon which its future depends.

The reflection of this grand strategy into Africa, which is now in its early stages, may largely grow out of the new Soviet political and economic offensive in the Middle East. Soviet broadcasts in several languages into Africa and particularly into North Africa are being increased. More and more young Africans are finding their way to the Soviet Union for study and training. Soviet representatives have been established in Libya and Ethiopia; a large delegation was present at the inauguration of President Tubman of Liberia and another has visited the Belgian Congo; Sudan was promptly recognized. It will be surprising indeed if these efforts are not steadily expanded.

Our success in strengthening our own influence in Africa will be measured by our ability to understand the nature of the challenge, to avoid panicky, negative reactions, and to devise a policy that serves our interests effectively and within our traditions.

Before World War II, a powerful navy, a staff of competent, tough-minded colonial administrators and relatively small forces of European-led "native" troops were sufficient to assure the colonial powers economic, political, and military domination over two-thirds of the world. Today, a sensitive diplomacy and the enlightened use of our economic advantages can alone enable America and her associates to substitute an enduring and mutually advantageous relationship with the dependent or formerly dependent peoples of Asia and Africa. Whether the Atlantic nations can muster the will and the skill to forge the necessary bonds while time is still on their side will, I believe, largely determine the shape and character of tomorrow's world.

III

The Response of the Colonial Powers

We have seen that the future of Africa is being shaped by three dynamic forces—(a) what I have described as the Revolution of Rising Expectations with its triple objective of political freedom, human dignity, and economic opportunity; (b) the crucial importance for the long haul of Asian and African raw materials to the growth, prosperity, and power of the United States and its European associates; (c) the global conflict between the Atlantic and Communist blocs.

Although the response of the European nations to these pressures varies greatly, a few generalizations are possible. But first I shall trace briefly how the European came to Africa.

No one can doubt that the attitude of the Western powers toward their African possessions, whatever its inadequacy to the problems we now face, is far more enlightened today than even a generation ago. To demonstrate this we need only to recall the cavalier way in which the European nations carved up Africa before and immediately after World War I.

Because there was enough to satisfy everybody, Africa was not even paid the compliment of being fought over. Instead, the partition of Africa became a relatively peaceful outlet for the conflicting ambitions of the European nations. In Africa, as Professor Harry R. Rudin of Yale has pointed out, "innocent victims were often sacrificed on the altars of international friendship."

The foundations of the Anglo-French entente of 1904, for instance, were laid when the French gave the British a free hand in Egypt in exchange for a free hand in Morocco. Neither the Egyptians nor the Moroccans, of course, were consulted.

After World War I, defeated Germany's African colonies were distributed among the victorious allies in accordance with the classic imperialist pattern. President Woodrow Wilson, however, secured reluctant acceptance of a mandate system through which the League of Nations placed modest restraints on the new guardians of these areas.

The disposition of Italy's African possessions after her defeat in World War II presented a more complex problem. Italy had been the last country to share in the partition of Africa, and hence its former colonial possessions—Libya, Eritrea, and Somaliland—are among the most barren and least productive.

The obvious solution would have been to place these colonies under the new United Nations trusteeship system. This, however, called for the selection of an administrating trust power. When the Soviet Union blandly offered its services, the Western powers decided that the best way out of the dilemma was to throw their support behind Libyan independence.

Thus the first nation in Africa to achieve independence after World War II was in fact one of the least prepared, economically and politically, for self-government. There was not even a respectable Libyan nationalist movement. Because of similar considerations, Somaliland, carved out of Italy's possessions on the eastern tip of Africa, and no better prepared than Libya, is to become independent in 1960 after ten years of Italian trusteeship.

Yet it is unfair to look on this innovation as a cynical reflection of the Cold War. In the last decade there has been a praiseworthy liberalization of colonial attitudes. In each of the three principal areas of Africa's aspiration—self-government, human dignity, and economic improvement—the changes, looking at the continent as a whole, have been spectacular. The reasons, however, why this progress has been less rapid than in Asia, where more than 600,000,000 subject people won their freedom in the same ten-year period, are complex and help to point up the difficulties which remain.

One purely African factor may be the absence of any surviving indigenous African civilizations to give the various nationalist movements the depth and confidence which the ancient cultures and religions of Asia have given Asian nationalism. In Asia the objective has been to recapture a glorious past, indeed to recapture freedom itself. This has given the struggle for self-government a special impetus and inspiration.

Egyptian civilization is, of course, one of the most

ancient in the history of man, but it belongs more to the Middle East than to Africa. The conquerors who built, developed, and rebuilt again the great cities and societies of Mediterranean North Africa were foreigners. The Phoenicians who founded Carthage were followed by the Romans, Vandals, Byzantines, Arabs, and finally the French and Italians.

On Africa's east coast and extending some miles inland, Arab centers of wealth and culture were created in the first centuries after Christ, and a flourishing trade existed with India and Southeast Asia. But the only indigenous African civilization was developed in West Africa.

The Ghana Empire, in what is now French West Africa and the Gold Coast, lasted from 300 A.D. until 1076, and was followed by the Mali empire, and then by the Songhai empire which was under strong Muslim influence and finally broke up in the sixteenth century. Timbuktu was at one time a highly cultured city with caravan connections as far east as Egypt, as far north as Tunis.

With the exception of the North African Mediterranean coast and East Africa bordering on the Indian Ocean, Africa was scarcely touched by the vigorous civilizations of Asia and Europe until the late fifteenth century. The European found the west coast of Africa virtually uninhabitable. Its climate was difficult, the natives hostile, good ports nonexistent, the rivers blocked by rapids only a few miles above their mouths, and its diseases deadly. These factors combined to set up formidable barriers to the exploration of the interior.

The Portuguese, and later the French, Dutch, and English, began their exploration of the African west coast in the late fifteenth century in search of a sea route to the wealth of Asia. The interior of West Africa and Central Africa were almost unknown by Europeans until the last half of the nineteenth century when Stanley and others traveled inland from the more hospitable eastern coast. It was the 1870's before the first European explorers, traveling down the broad Congo River, reached the point where the modern cities of Leopold-ville and Brazzaville stand today.

When World War II broke out, the nationalist movements of Asia were already vigorous and in a position to take full advantage of the political confusion and military weakness of the Western colonial powers. Nowhere in Africa, however, with the exception of the Gold Coast and Nigeria, had the nationalists developed sufficient organized following to create effective pressures for self-government.

In much of colonial Asia, moreover, boundaries reflected the historical divisions of former nations and empires which were often far older than Europe itself. The map of Africa, on the other hand, was drawn to reflect European convenience by more or less haphazardly combining and even dividing the 800 tribal areas.

But there was another difference which was of even greater direct importance. In the path of self-government in much of Africa is a hurdle which Asian nationalists rarely had to overcome: the stubborn, deeply entrenched, permanent white settlers.

WHEN INDEPENDENCE CAME TO INDIA, PAKISTAN, CEYLON, Burma, Indonesia, and the Philippines, following the war, there were probably no more than 200,000 Europeans and Americans living in all of Asia. Of these only a small minority were engaged in agriculture or otherwise in direct conflict with the Asians. Except in Indonesia, the majority were businessmen, civil servants, military officials, and educators who expected to end their days in Europe.

The contrast with Africa with its far smaller indigenous population is striking. Nearly 5,000,000 people of European origin consider Africa their permanent home. The outlook of most of these transplanted European-Africans is dominated by considerations which they believe to be basic to their personal security and which educated Africans consider diametrically opposed to their own.

Wherever the European presence in Africa is confined to those who generally consider themselves temporary residents—commercial representatives, missionaries, and colonial administrators—the transitions of this period are relatively smooth.

But wherever the Europeans have planted themselves on the land, they have created an explosive situation. Isolated from world realities, surrounded by an alien culture, insecure and vastly outnumbered, the white settlers have set up barriers to the economic, social, and political development of the Africans, regardless of their education or ability, that have created a void of bitterness. Thus their relations with the indigenous Africans and transplanted Indians among whom they have elected to spend their lives have deteriorated into a near impasse which often seems to defy rational solution.

The same pattern applies almost without exception throughout Africa. The larger the proportion of white settlers, the more explosive are the white man's relations with the Africans. The European settler arrogantly assumes the innate superiority of his race. As this assumed superiority becomes increasingly a mask for his growing insecurity and fear, so also it becomes increasingly insufferable to the black man.

The tragedy is reaching its climax in South Africa. It may be said that racial discrimination is as old as man, and its practice has not been confined to Europe and America. The African slave trade was dominated by Arabs; Japanese racial arrogance throughout Asia during the war was notorious; India's caste system is full of color overtones. Yet only in modern South Africa and Nazi Germany has racial superiority been made an official doctrine, sanctified by religion and philosophy, formalized by law, and institutionalized in the mores of a nation.

Precisely how the South African crisis may be solved is happily not within my scope here. Indeed, it is difficult to find informed observers who believe that a rational solution is still possible. The participants within the Union of South Africa appear to be caught in a suicidal cycle which may be fated to end in one of the ugliest explosions of violence in all history.

Because human relations based on a straight racist footing can be maintained only by force, the Afrikaners find themselves pledged to an ever-increasing degree of totalitarianism. This breeds an ever-increasing resentment from the nonwhites, which in turn creates even greater fear and more ruthless use of force from the Afrikaners. Today the Afrikaner extremist may be likened to a man who tries to put out the flames on his clothes by running faster and faster.

Can the flames be confined to South Africa? There

is no certainty. A bloody racial explosion in Johannesburg and Capetown would turn much of Africa against the white man, create new tensions in Asia and hasten the swing to communism throughout the world.

South Africa's general racial policies, her absorption of the League of Nations mandate of South-West Africa, and her treatment of the Indian minority have come before the General Assembly of the United Nations. The Union government has always opposed United Nations consideration of these problems on the grounds that they are domestic affairs outside the United Nations' jurisdiction. At the last session of the General Assembly, South Africa walked out and stayed out to emphasize its point.

Inevitably, relations within the British Commonwealth have been affected. Although Britain, Canada, Australia, and New Zealand do not condone South Africa's racial policies they support South Africa's view that the United Nations has no business discussing them. India, Pakistan, and Ceylon differ sharply.

Two years ago, South Africa made it clear that if the Gold Coast, following independence, becomes a member of the Commonwealth, it would withdraw. More recently, the South African government has appeared to retreat from this extreme position.

If South Africa should eventually leave the British Commonwealth, many observers point out that a source of friction and embarrassment would be removed. But on balance I cannot believe that the long-term result would be anything but destructive. Whatever moral restraint Britain and the rest of the Commonwealth can exercise on the racial extremists of South Africa would be weakened. It would mean the further isolation and deeper embitterment of the Afrikaner. This in turn would increase the sense of desperation among all other South Africans.

LET US NOW EXAMINE MORE CLOSELY HOW THE VARIOUS colonial powers are dealing with the specific problems that result from these pressures. Progress, as was indicated in the first chapter, varies widely. But is this progress rapid enough to meet the requirements of our time?

In British West Africa, the answer, barring unforeseen developments, is almost certainly "yes." Nowhere in Africa or Asia, except perhaps in Thailand, have I seen people so gay, relaxed, and unashamedly friendly toward white foreigners as in the Gold Coast. Here Africans have never come face to face with sovereignty on the basis of race, and the difference in their attitude is no less than spectacular.

Carrying forward its memorable record in India, Pakistan, Burma, Ceylon, Sudan, and now Malaya, the British in West Africa are moving with a high sense of responsibility toward the creation of new nations which, we can safely predict, will proudly take their place as members of the Commonwealth. Thus the inhospitable climate which discouraged British immigration to West Africa, plus the good sense of the British colonial administration, has made possible an experiment in self-government which holds much promise for all of Africa. Although their complex tribal conflicts will not be easy to reconcile, the African nations that are developing there have every prospect of success.

The real test of British statesmanship in Africa is taking place in the multiracial societies of Central and

East Africa. And here time is steadily running out. If the European and Asian minorities do not soon learn to live with the overwhelming Negro African majorities, all hope for political and economic stability may be lost. At the moment the outcome is hanging in the balance.

The Colonial Office in London is faced with a formidable task. It must take into account not only the interests of the African population, but the pressures of the white settlers, the relations of East and Central Africa with the rest of the continent, the rest of the Commonwealth, Asia, its implied pledges under the charter of the United Nations, and the world as a whole. The ways in which the British are striving to balance these forces can be most clearly seen in the Central African Federation.

The Federation, which was formed in 1953, consists of Southern Rhodesia, Northern Rhodesia, and Nyasaland, all situated just north of the Union of South Africa. Together they comprise an area more than twice as large as Spain with a population of 6,750,000.

Although the Europeans in the Federation number only 210,000, it is important to remember that this is more than all the Europeans in Asia in 1947. If present plans for increasing white immigration are carried out, the total will reach 1,000,000 by 1971.

Southern Rhodesia contains the largest white settlement. It is contiguous with South Africa and heavily influenced by it. Some 70,000 of Southern Rhodesia's 160,000 whites are of South African origin. Many of them are gripped by the spirit if not the letter of South African *apartheid,* and in deadly fear of both West African nationalism and Mau Mau terrorism.

Nyasaland has relatively few white settlers and although formal education is still rudimentary in most areas, its indigenous people are among the politically most conscious in Africa. Keenly aware of the strides their fellow Africans in the Gold Coast and Nigeria have been making toward complete independence, they fear the spread of South African *apartheid,* and they bitterly oppose the Federation as a backward step.

Somewhere in between, though much closer to Southern Rhodesia, is Northern Rhodesia. Although here the color bar is rigid, racial antipathy has not yet become pathological and there is reason to hope for an increasing degree of coöperation.

The British government had two reasons to push the Federation of these three areas: first, to move away from the costly and artificial balkanization of British Africa; second, to encourage potentially liberal counterforces which might gradually help to disengage Southern Rhodesia from the influence of South Africa.

The Central Federation government has a governor general, a prime minister, an Executive Council or Cabinet, and a federal Assembly. A majority of the 35 members of the Assembly are elected from an electorate restricted by property and education requirements. The six African members are either elected by an indirect system or appointed by the governor, as are the three Europeans who represent African interests. There is also an African Affairs Board which examines bills affecting African interests before they are submitted to the Assembly and has the right to appeal to London against legislation it regards as discriminatory.

The authority of the federal government includes defense, currency, income tax, customs and excise, civil aviation, health, and immigration. It is planned to increase the powers of the federal government gradually until the Federation becomes a dominion in the Commonwealth. In the meantime, the three component parts of the Federation retain their old legislative structures and much of their authority, including all legislation affecting the color bar.

Everyone agrees that the central african federation was evolved by men of ability and sincerity, and to the casual observer their handiwork sounds like the very incarnation of African colonial progress. Yet their program has met vigorous opposition from almost all quarters. Although many British argue that this is proof of its inherent fairness, an examination of the depth and character of the criticism will help us understand the complexity of the African-European relationships and give us some guides by which to judge the outlook for a solution which might be generally acceptable.

The authors of the plan are counting on the development of centrifugal forces that would create a strong multiracial nation strong enough to resist the nihilism of Mau Mau, the nationalism of Nkrumah, and the racism of Malan. During this process it was assumed that everybody in the Federation would give up something, and at the same time lose some part of his identity to the larger central concept. Although this makes a neat formula, there are many who question how well it works in practice.

Inevitably everybody is afraid that what he gives up will not be replaced by something equally valuable. Federation was opposed generally by the Bantu Africans, but most bitterly by the Nyasalanders who felt they had most to lose. With relatively few white settlers, they had looked forward to the emergence of Nyasaland as a proud and independent African nation enjoying friendly relations with the white man. This destiny, they argue, has been deliberately thwarted by their being thrown willy-nilly into a political melting pot where their cultural, racial, and national identity may be lost.

Since the riots in 1953, in which eleven lives were lost, Nyasalanders can hold political meetings only with the specific permission of the police. Yet the strength of the Nyasaland Africa Congress has grown steadily. Its principal spokesman, Wellington Chireva, M.P., insists that Nyasaland must become an "African state, the same as Uganda."

The African population of Northern Rhodesia, like that of Nyasaland, also looked forward to attaining self-rule as an essentially African state. As part of the Federation they felt that they were being removed from the friendly control of the Colonial Office and allowed gradually to slip under the domination of the white supremacy extremists of Southern Rhodesia.

Most Africans in all these areas deeply believe that the stated objective of multiracialism was a fraud. Instead of being a bulwark against *apartheid*, they were convinced that federation was an entering wedge through which it would be established. These African fears appeared to be confirmed by white settlers who have not hesitated to describe federation as a prudent move to head off more demanding forms of African self-government.

On the other hand there are many Europeans in Southern Rhodesia who argued that federation would swamp them with the numbers and nationalism of the Africans in the other two parts of the Federation. White skilled workers in the Rhodesias opposed the plan because they knew that their jobs would be threatened by any improvement in economic opportunities for the black Africans. Many transplanted Afrikaners and extremist Europeans who would like to free themselves entirely from the restraining influence of the Colonial Office in London also saw federation as a backward step.

South Africa's tough approach to race relationships has always had its share of admirers among the white settlers in Central and East Africa. "The time will come," they often say, "when we must cut loose from our British homeland, exactly as the European settlers in America did in 1776. After that we can deal with the African natives as the American settlers dealt with the American Indians." In addition to overlooking the presumably improved standards of twentieth-century governmental morality, they forget that the American settlers outnumbered the Indians by nearly ten to one, while in the Central African Federation the white settlers are outnumbered thirty-three to one by the Africans.

To these conflicting voices the British Colonial Office replies that each group must make its special interests secondary to the development of a strong nation with enough stability to make possible a peaceful, viable, multiracial society. Economic planning for the three countries as a whole, they say, is bound to mean faster development for the benefit of all.

To the Africans the British say that federation will inevitably mean a steady lowering of the color bar. The six Africans sitting in the new federal Assembly may still have little power, but their mere presence there represents a stunning defeat for white supremacists. Relations thus established in official life, it is said, are bound to spread to political, economic, and social spheres. Education will hasten this process.

The British government has already given some meaning to these claims. A three-year development plan is underway involving improvement of transport, power facilities, communications, and social services. The first university in the history of the Rhodesias is nearing completion in Salisbury, and it will be interracial although with segregated living quarters. At best it can be said that the outlook in general remains cloudy.

IN THE NORTHERN RHODESIA COPPER BELT THE WIDE differences in compensation and opportunity for advancement between white and African miners is one of the most dramatic and explosive examples of the color bar.

Yet in 1955, the two largest mining combinations reached an agreement with the white miners union under which twenty-four categories of jobs now held by white miners are to be opened to Africans, and studies will be made looking toward further advancement of Africans. Only a few hundred African workers will be affected, but any breach in the barrier, no matter how small, helps to weaken the entire structure.

It is a safe generalization that the owners and managers of enterprises such as the Rhodesian copper mines are willing to move faster in advancing the African miners than are the white miners. As long as there is no marked loss in efficiency, the greater the percentage of African miners the lower the operating costs—even though African wages are substantially raised.

It is the white worker, whose job status is directly threatened by the competition of the African worker, who is often the most vigorous champion of segregation. In the years of the Great Depression, this was a familiar phenomenon in the United States. As Africa moves toward industrialization, the pressures of the labor shortage will help break down many of the barriers precisely as it has done in America. This pressure is even beginning to be seen in South Africa.

The one problem on which there is little evidence of progress in either Central or East Africa is the alienation of the land from the African. One-half of the land of Southern Rhodesia, including practically all of the best land, is owned by the small European minority. Even in Nyasaland, where the land policy is far more equitable than in the Rhodesias and Kenya, the handful of white settlers own nearly a million acres of the best land. For years to come the pattern of land distribution will be the basis on which the overwhelming mass of Central and East Africans will form their attitude toward the European.

We can see even from this brief analysis that the creation of a genuine multiracial society with all the goodwill in the world and with governmental skill developed through generations of colonial experience is a formidable task. The Central African Federation will be under increasing racialist-nationalist pressure. The outcome remains in doubt.

IN BRITISH EAST AFRICA THERE HAS BEEN TALK OF ANother federation embracing Kenya, Tanganyika, and Uganda. However, because it implied that the two more liberal colonies, Uganda and Tanganyika, would be tied to settler-dominated Kenya, it was bitterly opposed by the Africans and finally dropped.

In 1955, the report of a British Royal Commission on the population, land, and economic problems of these three territories condemned the restriction of land use and ownership on the basis of race and urged the leasing of land without discrimination to those who could make the best use of it.

The Commission rejected the argument that East Africa suffers from overpopulation. All land, it recommended, should be utilized under carefully planned economic management. This would include teaching Africans modern agricultural, industrial, and business methods essential to raise African living standards. It would require a larger, not a smaller, population and open up broader economic opportunities for everyone.

This and other recommendations of the Commission are being studied by the Kenya Council of Ministers whose membership of sixteen includes two Indians and one African. No major decisions will be reached until after the elections scheduled for late in 1956 in which the white settlers choose between a party favoring the growth of multiracial government and one advocating something close to *apartheid*.

In all British territories of East and Central Africa there is the prospect of a gradual development toward multiracialism—in political authority, in human contacts, in economic opportunity. Africans are beginning to sit next to white men in legislatures, factories, and restaurants, and they are moving into the professions and government service.

Although the skilled African worker is a small minority, he can no longer be called a novelty. Lathe operators, welders, and mechanics are employed in significant numbers in the East African Railway and Harbour Administration; linotype operators and pressmen work in East African print shops. Trade schools for Africans exist and they are being expanded.

Yet many experienced observers believe that even in

Tanganyika and Uganda these changes are not keeping pace with African demands, that the moderate, democratically inclined African elite is losing its influence with the majority of Africans, and that the situation may ultimately reach the explosive stage. Even the stated objective of political multiracialism in Kenya with each of the three racial groups having an equal voice will not, they say, provide a lasting solution since it gives the European and Asian minority in combination a permanent veto power over the African majority.

Recently Sir Andrew Cohen proposed the direct elections, on a common roll regardless of race, of the representative members of Uganda's Legislative Council by 1961. The Uganda National Congress applauded the concept, but criticized the delays which in view of the enormous problems involved did not seem to be unreasonable.

The British in East, as in Central, Africa are faced with a complex and critical situation which will tax their wisdom and ingenuity to the utmost. Yet it is reassuring to remember that British flexibility has served in the past to keep almost equally difficult situations from getting totally out of hand. In addition to Pakistan, India, Burma, and Ceylon, there are West Africa, Egypt, Israel, and the Sudan as examples of Britain's capacity for imagination, resilience, and decisiveness under fire.

Many political scientists bemoan the apparent lack of order or logic in the British approach to colonial problems. Yet when political pressures force a transfer of power it is usually found that British faith in education and freedom of speech have somehow resulted in a cadre of able leaders, schooled in democratic procedures and prepared to govern.

The contrast between the political stability of the old British colonies in Asia and that of Indonesia which was under Dutch rule for 250 years, is pertinent. In India British-trained Indian civil servants and British-educated Indian leaders have been making extraordinary progress in creating a politically stable government and a steadily expanding economy. In Indonesia, the effort of the colonial Dutch to discourage political development and keep government functions in the hands of the Dutch and Eurasians has left a legacy of political and administrative inexperience.

A key to British success in India lies, I believe, in the system of education which, however glaring its inadequacies, opened up opportunities in government, business, the professions, and the military for the many thousands of young Indians who each year graduated from Indian or British universities. It may be too much to say that the British even now have a clearly planned educational policy for their African colonies. Yet British policy in Africa as in Asia is profoundly affected by two fundamental premises which are part of the Anglo-Saxon heritage: first, no intelligent man should be denied an education; second, no educated man should be denied the right to express his views.

Throughout British Africa these concepts are accepted in some measure. Even the most last-ditch European settlers do not wholly reject them. Consequently many able, persistent young Africans in the British possessions either now have or will soon have access to a university education.

This leads them to an understanding of democratic principles and a determination to put those principles to work. Eventually forces are set loose which challenge British colonial authority. So far, at least, when faced with forces which cannot be diverted from this purpose, the British have mustered the flexibility and skill to develop practical new relationships. As Gandhi once said, "An Englishman never respects you until you stand up to him; then he begins to like you."

This is reflected in a story that is told of Sir Andrew Cohen, able governor of Uganda, whose Executive Council had been asked to ratify the application for a Cambridge scholarship from one of the young African Congress leaders who had publicly denounced the governor's policies as "fascist." Sir Andrew, arguing vigorously for approval of the scholarship said: "If we are going to have political opponents—and I welcome them—let's at least take the pains to see that they are properly educated."

The educational facilities provided by the British in Africa vary, sometimes sharply, and from place to place. In Uganda, Sir Andrew has carried forward a broad well-planned educational system admirably fitted for Africa's needs.

When I visited Uganda in 1955, there were about 700 Africans taking training in engineering in brand-new technical schools where they were limited only by their ability to learn. Such a development would be deplored by the overpaid European miners in the Rhodesian copper belt who fear the competition of trained Africans as their forefathers feared the plague.

In Uganda there is also an East Africa multiracial university attended by 400 students from Uganda, Kenya, and Tanganyika where degrees are available in most fields including medicine. There is also a training center where some 400 village leaders and local administrators are given six-month training courses.

To expand its elementary education, Uganda has a teacher-training program underway which is scheduled to turn out 1,100 primary school teachers by 1959. Secondary school-teacher training is also in progress.

This is a respectable record for any underdeveloped nation of only five million population. In prewar colonial Africa, it would have been unthinkable.

Uganda's educational program, with its "leader" training, its emphasis on technical education, and its special effort to educate girls as well as boys, seems even better balanced than the impressive Gold Coast program. Yet no fewer than 3,000 Gold Coast students were studying in English-language institutions abroad last year. A new university for 1,000 students modeled on Cambridge and associated with London University has recently been completed.

I suggested to an official that this might create the same kind of maladjusted educational system in Africa that is now turning out so many frustrated intellectuals in India. The trouble in India, he answered, was not with the Cambridge-Oxford liberal-arts system but with the fact that India had allowed its standards to deteriorate. The Gold Coast University, he felt sure, would maintain the Oxford-Cambridge level, and its graduates eventually would build a free and democratic Africa.

Until secondary education is vastly improved, such standards will not be easy to maintain. Not enough well-prepared applicants are available, and so there are now many vacancies at the university.

Africa needs cultured, well-balanced leaders with the trained minds that can best be developed by a high standard liberal-arts education. But at this stage, if anything needs to be disproportionately stressed, it is the training of technical specialists.

Africa must be well governed. It must also be vigorously developed, and this can only be accomplished by a steady flow of engineers, doctors, and agricultural experts into government service and private practice.

Most observers agree that Asia and Africa could both do with fewer orators and more down-to-earth understanding of what needs to be done in the villages, hospitals, and industrial centers.

Yet whatever its lack of balance, the British respect for education offers the assurance that when independence finally comes there are usually leaders competent enough, wise enough, and balanced enough in their judgments to start the country on the path to a stable and enlightened future.

IN THE HEART OF AFRICA, SURROUNDED BY BRITISH, French, and Portuguese territories, is the great sweep of the Belgian Congo. The contrast between the Congo and its British and French neighbors on the question of settlers as on other subjects was put incisively by the governor general when I asked what it would take to put the Congo under Communist rule. His reply was: "One hundred thousand white European settlers."

I asked another Belgian official in the Congo what he would do if he were governor of Kenya. "I would float a loan," he replied, "buy the land, and move the white settlers out—even if it required all the NATO armies. If the settlers are allowed to keep control, they will bring all of Africa tumbling down about our ears."

The Belgians, as we have seen, have an intensely practical, no-nonsense attitude toward the Congo. Since the narrow interests of white settlers would conflict with the larger purposes of Belgium, there are few white settlers, and future white settlement is discouraged.

Yet there is plenty of opportunity for Belgians to make their fortunes in the Congo either by working or investing there. The central economic and political power as well is centered in five large commercial trusts which control 70 per cent of all the Congo's business.

Since self-government for the Congolese may threaten Belgian control of their economy, there is no promise of general elections, much less self-determination. In theory, the Belgians and educated Congolese will govern the Congo together. Development of the Congo requires the willing coöperation of the Congolese. They must share in the benefits. There must be no posturing about white supremacy on the one hand, and Africa for the Africans on the other.

The sophisticated Belgians know that the future strength and prosperity of their own country will ultimately depend on their ability to develop a Belgian-Congolese *partnership* in Africa. Belgium itself is a hard-working, European nation with a role in world affairs that is strictly limited by her small territory and her 8,000,000 people. But Belgium teamed with the vast, rich Congo and its 12,000,000 Africans can become an important and influential power. The Belgians are convinced that they are following the only sound path toward such a partnership.

At the United Nations conference in San Francisco in June, 1955, the Belgian foreign minister, Paul Henri Spaak, said, "This conference has fully convinced me that the complete equality of all races with all of its natural consequences has become a reality. Any contemporary statesman who refuses to admit this will make many mistakes."

In that same month, King Baudouin of Belgium, speaking at the Royal African Club in Brussels spelled out the steadily broadening political perspective of his Congolese government in encouraging new terms.

"It is not sufficient to endow this country with

wise social legislation and to improve the standard of living of its inhabitants. It is necessary that the whites and the natives achieve mutual understanding . . . and a happy society. A stable community must be built on the solid ground of tolerance . . . Then the moment will come—the date cannot yet be determined—to give our African territories a status which will guarantee for the happiness of all a true Belgo-Congolese community which will assure each one, black and white, the share that is due him according to his merits and capacity in the government of his country."

In referring to this important policy statement, a month later able Governor General L. Petillon before the Congo General Council expressed the conviction that "Segregation, or, in other words, discrimination, is not a solution. We reject this system. . . . Fusion or assimilation is a possibility," but, he thought, not the final answer because it could not be realized "on a large enough scale and because it would . . . result more in absorption than in fusion . . . in the substitution of western civilization for Bantu customs."

The final goal, he believed, was an association between a combination of Belgians and educated Congolese on the one hand and Congolese people on the other.

"Such an association," he continued, "implies certain reciprocal rights and privileges. We non-natives and assimilated natives will have ours; they will have theirs."

Nearly 50 per cent of all Congolese children of primary-school age already attend schools and this percentage is growing steadily. Although most schools are run by Catholic missions with government subsidies,

83

there are now 2,000 Protestant missionaries there, half of them American.

After primary school a Congolese may learn to become a highly skilled carpenter, an accountant, a medical assistant, or a pharmacist. Education is planned in medicine, agriculture, the liberal arts, and eventually engineering—but not law. The Belgians have noted that the most able nationalist leaders in British Africa received their training at the bar.

Although the new university now being constructed outside Leopoldville is small, it is interracial and its standards are high. The number of Congolese studying in Belgium is less than twenty.

FRENCH POLICY IN AFRICA IS EASIER TO ASSESS. SO FAR as it has been based on the hope that Africans would become assimilated as Frenchmen, it has turned out to be, on the whole, a failure.

There have been some small successes in West and Equatorial Africa, particularly among the Senegalese and in military affairs. Here where the French settlers are few in number, political progress has also been encouraging. There has also been some adoption of French culture by the Tunisians.

But the bulk of North Africa's Arab and Berber Muslims have remained altogether impervious to assimilation. In fact, the French with their legitimately great traditions, their concept of themselves as "civilizers," and their mild racial attitudes, have found themselves faced with more violent opposition than any other European power in Africa.

How completely assimilation has broken down was dramatized in the elections for a new French National

Assembly held in January 1956. In what is presumably the largest section of Metropolitan France, Algeria, no election was held because of an "exceptional" situation. This "exceptional" situation grew out of the fact that Algerian terrorists threatened death not only to members of the electorate, but also to any person, French or Muslim, who was foolhardy enough to stand for election.

After 125 years of French rule in Algeria, only one-sixth of the Algerian children of school age go to school. This, the Algerians say, can hardly be considered proper preparation for the exercise of a free franchise.

The French government now realizes that it must eventually come to terms with whatever responsible Algerian leaders may emerge or suffer a debacle similar to that in Indochina. Yet its difficulties are compounded, on the one hand, by the fact that because of the stubborn refusal to compromise earlier Algerian nationalism has largely fallen under the sway of violent Islamic extremists, and on the other, by the presence of what by now we recognize as Africa's greatest obstacle to racial harmony—1,200,000 stubborn French settlers, many of whom belong to families who have lived in Algeria for a hundred years. Here we find the same familiar cycle: too little self-government grudgingly granted creates new pressures which lead to the cry of all or nothing.

In Tunisia and Morocco, where French accomplishments in the tradition of Marshal Lyautey have been substantial, the point of no return has been reached and passed, and the French government has wisely, if belatedly, faced up to this fact. In 1955 a large degree of internal autonomy was achieved by the nationalists of both countries, and independence—perhaps within a newly defined French Union—will soon become a fact.

Although this represents a decisive defeat for the assimilationists and for those who assumed that a permanent French-dominated connection between France and North Africa was attainable, it is a victory for the growing number of Frenchmen who support an approach in line with France's great liberal tradition.

The convention giving Tunisia internal autonomy was signed on June 3, 1955. The nationalist movement was persuasively and effectively led by Habib Bourguiba, president of the Neo-Destour party of Tunisia, who until recently had been a French prisoner although an ardent anti-Communist, a supporter of the Western alliance, an admirer of French culture, as well as an advocate of an independent and democratic Tunisia.

Bourguiba faced opposition from the far more extreme Salah Ben Youssef, the former secretary general of Neo-Destour (not to be confused with the sultan of Morocco), who was ousted when the party failed to support his demand for total independence at once. But this time the French acted before the situation got out of hand; elections were held in the winter of 1956, and Bourguiba won a sweeping victory. The extremists of Left and Right won only a small fraction of the total vote.

The concept of assimilation died in Morocco on December 7, 1955, when the first Moroccan cabinet in history took office. Of the sixteen ministers, seven were members of Istiqlal, the nationalist party which the French had outlawed from the time of its formation.

Except for ministers of defense and foreign affairs, the new cabinet covered the full range of governmental authority. This authority was taken over, not only from the French but also from the viziers of the sultan who agreed to the transformation from a nominally absolute to an actually constitutional monarchy. Just before this

86

cabinet was sworn in, the Istiqlal party held a congress and adopted as its aim a fully independent, unified and democratic Morocco. On March 3, 1956, in a joint French-Moroccan declaration, France solemnly recognized the independence of Morocco subject to the conclusion of new agreements govering their future relationship as equals. Two months later these final agreements were signed and Morocco emerged, to all intents and purposes, as an independent nation.

Spain has accepted these developments with imagination and dignity. During his exile by the French, the Spanish government continued to recognize the sovereignty of the sultan. In April, 1956, it promised full independence for Spanish North African territories as part of a united Morocco. The swift pace of these developments in Morocco and Tunisia is encouraging.

Moroccans and Tunisians will need outside assistance for some time, and this assistance should logically come from France. But a nationalism that has triumphed through violent pressure may be reluctant to accept help from the former colonial power for very long. Until some means is found to break the bloody impasse in Algeria, the situation throughout North Africa will remain unsettled.

France's many earnest admirers can justly point to the construction of excellent highways, handsome cities, and extensive irrigation projects in North Africa. But they will also agree that the French might have done far more to prepare North Africans for self-government.

In the administration of Morocco in 1955 the French held 5,500 top executive jobs and the Moroccans 165. The ratio was about the same in the professions. As in South Vietnam, the French still controlled the bulk of

Morocco's industrial and commercial life and occupied almost all key managerial posts.

In French West Africa and French Equatorial Africa with their combined population of more than 20,000,000 we find a far different kind of situation. Here, as in British West Africa, there are few Europeans, and the atmosphere is correspondingly free from tension. Relationships between Africans and French officials are generally good. Considerable progress has been made toward free elections. Yet, as in North Africa, the desire for self-determination is strong, and eventually it must prove decisive.

In 1946 the vigorous Rassemblement Democratique Africaine (African Democratic Movement) was tagged as a Communist movement and in 1949 it was largely crushed by the French authorities. In 1956, purged of its extremist faction, it emerged again as a powerful rallying point for nationalist sentiment.

Thus we may expect to see the independence movement grow steadily in French Africa south of the Sahara as well as north of it. We may also expect to see strong support for a federal association of French African territories under a single government.

Let us hope that here as well as in North Africa some valuable lessons have been learned. The old thought that independence can be postponed indefinitely simply by preventing colonial peoples from learning how to handle their own affairs has had its costly consequences.

When independence does come—and under such circumstances it usually comes with a rush—lack of preparation puts a heavy burden on the responsible leaders who could normally be counted upon to maintain a friendly relationship with the former colonial power. When, as often happens, these leaders are unable to satisfy their people, they are replaced as in Algeria with extremists who insist on a total break.

Indonesia's present embittered relations with the Netherlands is a dreary illustration of this now familiar cycle and a contrast with the cordial relations which exist between the United Kingdom on the one hand, and India, Pakistan, Ceylon, and Burma on the other.

IN PORTUGUESE AFRICA—ANGOLA AND MOZAMBIQUE— the cycle which I have described is in its earliest stages, but the pressures for self-determination will sooner or later be felt. Through the system of assimilation, as we have seen, those Africans who have attained certain educational, economic, and cultural levels are given the full rights and privileges of the white man. There is little outward evidence of a color bar.

Yet only about 30,000 Africans in Angola and 5,000 in Mozambique have achieved this status. The rest of the 9,000,000 Africans under Portuguese control are outside the pale of the rights for civilized man.

One of the outstanding injustices on the African continent is the Portuguese system of forced labor, which is referred to as "directed labor." This system is a logical outgrowth of Portugal's postulate that every man has a moral duty to work. Under its operation native recruiters go out into the villages and round up the necessary number of men for work on the big plantations. The "directed" laborers are those who have failed to work voluntarily for a certain annual period according to the Portuguese Labor Code. After deduction of taxes and assessments from their wages, these forced workers have practically nothing left.

Now that Portugal is a member of the United Nations

it will be possible to focus more international attention on a system that appears second only to the Union of South Africa in its harsh treatment of the Africans.

Of the three objectives of the revolution of rising Expectations, it may be said that relatively the easiest to achieve is the first—self-government. This involves a direct, easily understood and mechanical operation—namely getting rid of the foreign ruler. The results are clearly visible. The achievement of the second and third aims—human dignity and economic advancement—is much more complex and in many ways will always be more difficult.

Because the desire for freedom from foreign rule is such a powerful elemental urge, and because nationalist movements are so strongly favored by world forces, we may assume that sooner or later and by one means or another Africa's dependent areas will gain their independence. But the means by which freedom is achieved will go far to determine the stability, character, and survival power of the new African states.

For most awakened Africans, as we have seen, education is the touchstone of their future. Although their passionate faith in education is based partly on an understandable appreciation of what education can do, it also has psychological and political overtones.

The white man came to Africa as master. The white man could read, write, multiply and divide. As the black man learns to do these things he assumes that he will take his place beside the white man. When racial obstacles are then placed in his way an explosive situation is created.

The speed and character of economic development

may be almost equally important. In theory the wisdom of such development is no longer an arguable proposition anywhere in the world, but for the future stability of Africa it has a special significance. Inevitably political emancipation in the eyes of the colonial peoples carries with it the assumption of economic emancipation.

As African colonies win their independence they will be faced with unrealistic demands from their people and only a limited time in which to meet them. They will be harried by their own fellow-African landlords, tax collectors, lawyers, and entrepeneurs, many of whom will be at least as ruthless in their methods of exploitation as the Europeans. The most impoverished people I saw in all Africa were share croppers on a coffee estate belonging to an educated African.

On such matters newly independent governments will be particularly vulnerable to the Communists. The classic formula for violent revolution involves three ingredients: the growth of an underprivileged, urbanized group of workers, peasants working the land of others, and a frustrated, educated elite.

The interest of a retiring colonial power in leaving behind an economically healthy colony and a politically viable people is therefore more than humanitarian. It is basic to continuing friendly and profitable relations and to the strategic interest of the Atlantic nations. For these purposes, an economically healthy colony means one whose resources are clearly being developed for the needs of Africans as well as Europeans.

One of the most impressive achievements of the Europeans in colonial Africa, as in Asia, is the growth of transportation and communications. The contrast with Ethiopia and Liberia which have been traditionally independent and which still have practically no railways of their own is striking. These facilities are essential to a sound economy and will undoubtedly be of great long-range benefit to Africa; but they have not yet produced much immediate income for the African.

Most of Europe's economic exertions in Africa continue to be devoted to developing primary mineral and agricultural products for export. This serves the Europeans well. It will also serve the Africans well once they begin to participate as more than underpaid laborers. For some years to come, the additional investment required for the development of resources for internal needs must come from the Atlantic nations. But more and more it will be accepted only to the extent that it clearly creates a better life for the Africans.

An excellent example of enlightened management has been recently provided by an American firm, the Liberian Mining Company, closely associated with American steel interests. When it was determined that the Bomi deposits in Liberia were far richer than it had been assumed, this company volunteered to scrap the contractual agreement and to provide a far greater return to the Liberian government and its people. Such actions provide the solid basis for enduring partnerships. On this score the record of American companies in Africa, including South Africa, has been generally good.

Constructive and imaginative economic enterprises are not lacking in today's Africa. In the Gold Coast, for instance, the export of cocoa has been organized with great skill to provide an effective economic base for the country's development and stability. Now to offset dependence on this one commodity, the vast Volta River development will soon be undertaken primarily to provide the power for one of the world's greatest aluminum producing centers. Likewise, the Belgian Congo's ambitious ten-year plan envisions a $960,000,000 investment by 1959—44 per cent of this in transportation development. In one way or another most colonial areas are now moving ahead in the economic field, some of them with extraordinary rapidity.

All African colonial powers have projects aimed at expanding the internal markets of their colonies. Some of these projects are vigorously underway. Yet by far the largest economic group has been largely neglected: the farmer. With a little land of his own, some fertilizer, new simple tools, and, in some cases, irrigation, he could feed himself better, grow a cash crop, begin to buy a few things in the nearby town, achieve a new sense of security, and thus create increasing stability and prosperity in the African countryside. Here, as elsewhere, Africa has much to learn from India.

IN THIS CONTINENT OF 193,000,000 AFRICANS, 5,000,000 Europeans, and 600,000 Asians, it is clear that a great awakening is taking place. The people of Africa, like the people of underdeveloped countries everywhere, have glimpsed what their life could be like if modern science were put to work for their benefit.

More and more Africans are also becoming particularly aware of the wealth that lies in their soil. They sense the growing dependence of the Western world and of the United States in particular on their mineral resources. They are beginning to see that this dependence gives them increased leverage to carry forward their revolution in the context of the Cold War. They are pondering the Communist accusation that the West's current interest in Africa involves no more than a crude transition from slavery in the last century to uranium in this.

93

The reaction of the colonial powers in Africa to these new pressures varies, from the enlightened liberalism of the British in West Africa to the outworn colonial concepts of the Portuguese in Angola and Mozambique. May it not be said that this variation in colonial technique reflects the degree of confidence that each colonial power has in itself and in its own future?

During the war, the British brilliantly demonstrated their courage and greatness. Their liberal postwar colonial policies have seemed to reflect this inner confidence. The Portuguese on the other hand seem to be clinging to an imperial glory which has lost its reality.

Although the pace, methods, and ultimate objectives vary widely, constructive changes are taking place throughout Africa. Yet the more pessimistic observers wonder if the African's mistrust of the European has not reached a stage where, regardless of what is said or done, he simply will not believe Europe's improved intentions toward him; whether, in other words, it is not already too late to form the essential partnership.

Although it would be reckless to discount this grim possibility, there is reason, I believe, to hope for a more constructive result. Clearly the United States has not only a profound interest in that result, but a contribution to make in its development.

IV

An American Approach to Africa

In this final chapter I shall suggest in broad outline an American approach toward Africa. This is not an easy assignment, and I undertake it with considerable humility. The situation throughout most of Africa is extraordinarily complex and it is difficult to touch any phase of it without treading controversial ground where honest men hold widely divergent opinions.

Despite Africa's new importance in global affairs and our own deepening involvement in its fate, these complexities have helped to convince many American officials that our policy should be to have no positive policy at all. Because Africa is largely dominated by our European allies, it is said that open opposition to African colonialism has become a luxury that America can no longer afford.

This argument reflects a conviction that the survival of Western civilization has come to depend not on the principles which give it meaning and direction, but on the ability of the descendants of Locke, Rousseau, and Jefferson to counter the interrelated political, economic, military, and ideological challenge which it now faces by a predominantly *military* policy of containment.

Even under cursory analysis this argument, it seems to me, quickly falls apart. Our traditional stand on self-determination conflicts in no sense with the requirements of military security; indeed, our national-security objectives and the objectives of responsible African nationalists closely coincide.

What these new African leaders want most from us now is the responsible reassertion of the democratic principles which have provided the primary energizing force behind America's growth and influence. Because of our failure to recognize this fact, we have been allowing what should be an opportunity to become a quandary.

By now we have seen enough of the political realities of Africa to know that the pace of events there can no longer be controlled by our European friends. Although we cannot control it either, wise policies may enable us to influence developments in ways that will advance the aspirations of the Africans, and protect not only our legitimate interests, but also those of our NATO allies.

But our present policy of negativism is dissipating any capacity we may have to fulfill this constructive function. The most powerful nation in the world, which asserts that it is leading a global coalition for freedom, cannot declare itself to be a nonparticipant in the affairs of a continent boiling with change, without abdicating its position of leadership.

It is in the United Nations that our pretense of being able to get along without a positive and constructive African policy collapses completely. The principal organs of the United Nations have become increasingly concerned with precisely those problems that gave rise to the Revolution of Rising Expectations. In the 1955 session of the General Assembly, questions arising out of traditional European colonialism held the center of the stage. Thus Africa, the last great area of such colonialism, was in the spotlight most of the time.

In determining whether we believe Morocco, Tunisia, and Algeria to be proper topics for discussion in the General Assembly we are forced to reveal some estimate of the situation in North Africa. We are forced to indicate some kind of attitude toward the problem of racial strife in general and discrimination against South Africa's Indians in particular. We must have something, however tentative, to say on South-West Africa.

In the Committee on Information from Non-Self-Governing Territories, we are also forced—if only by silence—to reveal a political outlook. Likewise, the positions we take in the Economic and Social Council and in the specialized agencies indicate to sensitive Asian and African ears and eyes how alert we are—or how indifferent—to the economic, educational, and human problems of Africa.

But it is in the Trusteeship Council that we are forced most directly to come to grips with African problems. The bulk of the United Nations' trust territories lie in Africa. They comprise, excluding South-West Africa, seven political units covering a land area equal to New

97

England and the Middle Atlantic states, containing some 17,500,000 people.

Yet to say that the United States must formulate some kind of policy on trusteeship matters merely because we are members of this Council, is an inadequate statement of our responsibilities. Our involvement is far deeper rooted. For without us the concept of trusteeship probably would never have been translated into practical operation.

The lineal ancestor of the Trusteeship Council is the League of Nations' mandate system which first sought to establish the principle of international accountability for dependent areas. It was Woodrow Wilson who insisted that the mandate system should be incorporated into the League Covenant. He succeeded after a difficult struggle against our wartime allies who had accepted his Fourteen Points as the basis for peace. It was Secretary of State Cordell Hull who picked up the Wilsonian concept in 1943 and, with the support of Franklin Roosevelt, began to press for the creation of what became the United Nations Trusteeship Council.

Today Asians, Africans, and people everywhere who were brought up to believe that this system was among the more constructive achievements of American statecraft watch in despair as we sit in the Trusteeship Council, squirming our way through some of the most important issues of our time, and seeking to convince ourselves that the domination of one people by another is not really our affair unless the "other" is the Soviet Union.

When seen in the light of our responsibilities in the United Nations, the conviction of many American leaders that we cannot afford a more constructive African policy seems shortsighted. In the expanded United Nations with its seventeen new members, most of which can be counted upon to take strongly anticolonial positions, it may be ruinous.

Let me add another practical consideration. In French North Africa, mainly Morocco, we have invested more than one half billion dollars in air and naval bases. The narrow school of statesmanship which believes that military policy is the sum and substance of foreign policy has consistently used the security of these bases as its main argument for opposing any proposal that we develop a more sensitive approach to African nationalism.

This reasoning disregards some of the most fundamental facts of our time. No trend in Africa is clearer than the steady reduction of French power and the inexorable rise of the North African nationalists. With each passing day, the fate of our bases has become more dependent on groups whose opinions and aspirations we have largely ignored.

Because military thinking has so dominated our foreign policy we have felt compelled to support the French position that Algeria is part of France in the face of vigorous opposition to this view not only in Algeria, but in Morocco and Tunisia. North Africans are keenly aware that the French troops who pursue the Algerian nationalist guerillas through the hills are equipped with American small arms, artillery, tanks, planes, and helicopters given them under the NATO agreement.

Morocco is now on the threshold of complete independence. On January 17, 1956, Mohammed Cherkaoui, Minister of State in the new government, pointed out that our vast military establishment there had been authorized by the French in 1950 without consultation with the Sultan

99

or his people. His tone was not unfriendly, but the implications were clear. The future status of our bases, he said would be decided not in Paris but in Rabat.

In the April, 1956, issue of *Foreign Affairs* Ahmed Balafrej, the new Moroccan foreign minister, asked bluntly: "Did France have the right to dispose of part of the land under her protection to a third party? Did she have the right to hand over the use of it . . . without obtaining the consent of those primarily concerned—the Moroccans?"

Our stubborn failure to recognize the new sources of power in Africa and Asia has long been deplored by some American military leaders, but such critics are rare. In 1955, for instance, General James Van Fleet sharply criticized our "adherence to antiquated European colonial policies." Instead, he believed we should take an independent road consistent with our own statements and principles. No military base, he said, no matter how powerful or well guarded, is of much use if it stands "as an island surrounded by a hostile sea."

Questions of this kind apply not only to military bases but also to the most intensely practical of all considerations regarding Africa—raw materials. We have seen how American industry, in war or peace, is increasingly dependent on certain key African minerals. If the simmering South African volcano should erupt or the tricky balance of forces in the Congo break down, our position in the nuclear-jet age could be mortally threatened. If practical American policy is to extend beyond the arrival of the next shipload of cobalt, columbite, or pitchblende from Africa, such factors must be taken into account.

At present the world is not even giving us credit for a deliberate policy of minding our own business in Africa.

100

What seems to us a policy of benevolent noninvolvement appears to others as indecision. Many leaders of the colonial powers regard us as blundering sentimentalists, while many African nationalists charge us with being timid hyprocrites. Instead of making friends in each group, we are antagonizing both, without winning the respect of either.

On V-J Day we stood before the people of the now uncommitted world as the champions of individual rights and opportunities, the most powerful and respected member of the Grand Alliance which had broken the power of the race-conscious Nazi and Japanese imperialists and had given freedom still another chance. If we allow the reality to be drained from that image, we will sooner or later lose our ability to influence the course of history in half the world. If such is the result of trying to avoid taking a position on African questions, it is hard to see how we could do worse by adopting a more constructive approach. But the argument need not be based on these negative grounds. The positive reasons for a new outlook on Africa are in themselves compelling, and we start out with advantages that are greater by far than those of any other nation.

AFRICANS STILL DRAW INSPIRATION FROM OUR HISTORY of anticolonialism, in spite of the violence which many of our policy makers have done to this tradition. The words that Americans have used generation after generation to describe their dedication to the goal of human freedom in all parts of the world are well known to most educated Africans. It may be worthwhile to review some of these words in the context of the present-day African revolution.

Our Declaration of Independence said that "all men are created equal." Its author, Thomas Jefferson, believed that "all eyes are opening to the thoughts of man . . . the mass of mankind was not born with saddles on their backs, nor a favored few, booted and spurred, ready to ride them by the grace of God." Under extreme circumstances he did not hesitate to support violence: "The tree of liberty," he once said, "must be refreshed from time to time with the blood of patriots and tyrants."

Tom Paine spoke of the "small spark kindled in America" that is not to be extinguished. Washington was certain that democracy throughout the world was "finally staked on the experiment attributed to the American people," and remarked that he felt "irresistibly excited whenever in any country I see an oppressed people unfurl the banner of freedom." His successor, John Adams, said that the development of American democracy was the "opening of a grand scene and design of Providence for the emancipation of the slavish part of mankind all over the earth."

"The right of revolution," said Lincoln, "is a most sacred right; a right which we believe is to liberate the world." Our revolution, he thought, would ease the lot of peoples "over a great portion of the globe." A few years later General Ulysses Grant spoke of the sympathy of the American people for all those "who struggle for liberty and self-government."

Thus Wilson's Fourteen Points in 1917 with their advocacy of the rights of self-government for subject people were deeply rooted in the American tradition. When he called for "a free, open-minded and impartial adjustment of all colonial claims," his words again carried a familiar and respected American principle into the most remote corners of the world.

Even the resentment with which many European political leaders viewed Wilson's support of self-determination had its counterpart in earlier days. Nearly a century earlier Austrian Foreign Minister Metternich had charged America with "fostering revolutions wherever they show themselves, in regretting those which failed and extending a helpful hand to those which prosper."

With Franklin D. Roosevelt America's anticolonial tradition was further reinforced. His Four Freedoms were specifically earmarked for "everywhere in the world" as were the words of the Atlantic Charter which included "the right of all peoples to choose the form of government under which they will live."

In June, 1955, the Congress of the United States, sensing the degree to which our government had strayed from these frequently professed convictions, took the unusual step of restating what it assumed to be our position. After speaking of our traditional support of other peoples in their operations to achieve self-government, Congress in a concurrent resolution said: "It is the sense of the Congress that the United States should administer its foreign policies and programs and exercise its influence so as to support other peoples in their effort to achieve self-government or independence under circumstances which will enable them to assume and maintain an equal station among the free nations of the world."

So what the African people expect of us today is not a departure from our tradition but a reaffirmation of it. These words, they tell us, either mean what they say or else they represent a vast hypocrisy. When harried American policymakers suggest that under present-day conditions such principles as self-determination are valid in some years and not in others, or that they apply to white Poles but not to dark-skinned Africans, the dis-illusionment of the people in Asia, Africa, and indeed throughout most of the world, is profound. They judge us no longer to be dealing in principles, but in propaganda, and they ask bluntly how Americans can honestly claim that the morality of Washington is superior to that of Moscow.

Our tradition of anticolonialism, however, is not the sum total of our ideological advantages in Africa. We not only achieved our independence, but we went on to base our development on the solid foundation of human dignity and opportunity and to create an extraordinarily prosperous economy, the fruits of which have been broadly shared. To all the millions of Africans marching in the Revolution of Rising Expectations this record can become a genuine and shining inspiration.

If what *Fortune* magazine calls the Permanent American Revolution is the continuing historical process that encourages many African nationalists in their struggle for self-government, human dignity, and expanding economic opportunities, the text that inspires them directly or indirectly is the Bible. We have seen that about one-eighth of the people of Africa are Christian. Whatever education exists in Africa has been largely the work of Christian missions. There is hardly an African leader south of the Sahara who has not attended a Christian school.

The interest of many African leaders in such revolutionary ideas as individual liberty, the potential dignity and capability of all men, and, through an inevitable process of logical extension, self-government has its source in the Christian faith. Thus the Christian missionaries and their Book have been in this very practical sense Africa's true revolutionaries.

These Biblical concepts, deeply rooted in the nature of man, are more valid, more lasting, more pervasive than anything Africans can find in Karl Marx's *Das Kapital*. By continuing to cherish them, African leaders have every reason to hope that over the years they can create free societies invulnerable to totalitarian rule. By following the contemporary disciples of Marx, Africans would simply exchange an old tyranny for a new. Again this reflects our American involvement in Africa, a deeply spiritual involvement that cannot lightly be rationalized out of existence, and which is dramatized by the presence of 4,500 American missionaries in Africa.

If Christianity transcends nationality, then serious Christians in America must be concerned with the Christian effort in Africa regardless of the nationality of the missionaries or the color of the faithful. Indeed, serious Christians must be concerned with the condition of man, whatever his faith; otherwise, their faith is a sham. Precisely what this concern involves lies within the conscience of each Christian.

Beyond the ties of security, tradition, and religious faith is the American Negro. African Negroes came to America involuntarily; but they came—in one of the many waves of immigration that has given the United States its multiracial character. During the last half of the eighteenth century, the annual rate of the slave traffic has been estimated at 100,000.

Today one of every ten Americans has an African ancestor. In this sense we have closer ties to Africa than has any nation in Europe. Among the many "homelands" that exert a pull on our various national groups, Africa, at least West Africa, ranks with the rest as a part of our rich national background. Anyone who has listened to the music and watched the dancing of a West African village will recognize many of the familiar rhythms of Martinique and Mississippi.

From its earliest days the African slave trade was opposed, however ineffectually, in the United States, and this fact gave rise to a complementary involvement with Africa. One hundred and sixty years ago, Benjamin Franklin worked unceasingly for the abolition of African slavery and collaborated with French and British philosophers in an effort to create self-governing nations in Africa.

It was the American conscience that established Liberia as a home for emancipated slaves as early as 1822 and gave it a capital named Monrovia in honor of President James Monroe. Abraham Lincoln is still a hero and inspiration to Africans, and it is no accident that brings modern African leaders such as Kwame Nkrumah, prime minister of the Gold Coast, and Dr. Azikiwe, prime minister of the Eastern Region of Nigeria, to study at Lincoln University outside Philadelphia. Such connections give a special dimension to our relations with Africa and indeed with the entire crucial underdeveloped world.

When Europeans fail to support their nationalist aims, few Africans are surprised for the European is the traditional colonial adversary. But the African nationalist who encounters indifference, temporizing, or opposition from Americans is angered and disillusioned. Because so much more is expected of us, we are the more bitterly criticized when we disappoint.

Thus, it may be said that we have a clear moral, ideological, and—one might say—historical responsibility to play a constructive role in Africa or repudiate one of the most basic elements in our American heritage.

And most Africans still believe that we will recognize that role and play it to the hilt.

The many-sided American ideological involvement in Africa which I have described will undoubtedly be dismissed as irrelevant to the present conflict by that school of diplomacy which places its faith primarily in military measures. With this I cannot agree.

In earlier days when national power could be defined almost exclusively in terms of geography, alliances, well-drilled professional armies, able generals, productive capacity, and skilled diplomacy, their narrow view of *Realpolitik* had considerable validity. But in today's interrelated, revolutionary world it is as outmoded as the Maginot Line.

If Moscow, Peking, and recent Asian and Middle Eastern history have taught us anything, they have demonstrated that in our era of fast communications, increasing literacy, and rising aspirations such factors as people, ideas, and faith are emerging as major and often decisive components of national power. Moral considerations, always fundamental in shaping individual human behavior, have, therefore, become crucial elements in determining relationships between whole peoples. Of one thing I am sure: if American foreign policy continues to fly in the face of these ideological forces, it will ultimately come to grief.

Yet the slogans of freedom, however frequently or skillfully expressed on the Voice of America or in official statements, will not in themselves prove adequate. A false return to our revolutionary tradition for tactical purposes will certainly fail. America will be judged by the world jury, and her global influence correspondingly weakened or strengthened, by our day-today *performance* on the issues which now move much of mankind.

Although the arguments for negativism do not appear persuasive, it would be reckless to deny the magnitude of the difficulties and the complexity of the decisions which brought this negativism into being. Let us proceed, however, to sketch, if we can, what needs to be done and how we may move toward a position that is positive and yet responsible.

It is clear by now that an enlightened American approach to Africa must take primary account of the Revolution of Rising Expectations which is being generated throughout Africa—north, south, east and west. Although formal diplomacy is not an ideal instrument for dealing with dynamic social forces, there are other channels legitimately available to us; and even if we cannot deal with these forces directly, we can at least take them into account.

Our day-to-day approach, as I see it, should be flexible and yet based on long-term consideration. The general direction of the African revolution is quite clear. In some areas it is moving more quickly than in others, and in these areas it is likely to break out into headlines and crises that may tempt us into makeshift and unsatisfactory action. As far as possible we must anticipate these inevitable crises. Although our objectives should be generally applicable, they should be so devised that they may be carried forward at speeds adjusted to particular conditions.

For the framework of an American policy toward Africa we can do no better, I believe, than to turn to Secretary of State Cordell Hull whom so much of the world respected for his unique combination of crackling practicality and mellow wisdom. Mr. Hull's views on colonialism were responsible and deeply rooted in the American tradition. During World War II he foresaw both the rapid growth of nationalism in Africa and Asia and the power of the revolutionary movements which it would generate. Toward the end of his memoirs, written in 1949, Mr. Hull said:

"Our great nation should stand always for the progressive attainment of self-government and eventual independence by dependent people when they are ready for it, in accordance with our example in the Philippines. But let our policy in this respect not be limited to one of exhortation only."

As a student of the failure of our Open Door policy to discourage aggression in China and the disappointments of the Wilson era, Mr. Hull had learned that exhortation in dealing with complex global problems has its own strict limits of effectiveness. In the discussion preliminary to the development of the United Nations, Mr. Hull pressed upon the British in particular, who he felt were most likely to respond positively, a series of five principles which he proposed should guide the colonial powers in their postwar relationships with Africa and Asia. His statement of principles included the following:

"First, they were to give the colonial peoples protection, encouragement, moral support, and material aid, and to make continuous efforts towards their political, economic, social and educational advancement.

"Second, they were to make available to qualified individuals among the colonial peoples, to the fullest possible extent, positions in the various branches of the local governmental organizations.

"Third, they were to grant progressively to the colonial people such measures of self-government as they were capable of maintaining in the light of their various stages of development towards independence.

"Fourth, they were to fix at the earliest practicable moment dates on which the colonial peoples would be accorded the status of full independence within the system of general security.

"Fifth, they were to pursue policies under which the natural resources of colonial territories would be developed, organized and marketed in the interests of the people concerned and of the world as a whole."

These farsighted proposals were greeted with scant enthusiasm among our European associates. Yet they formed in large measure the thinking behind Chapters XI, XII and XIII of the United Nations Charter which relates to trusteeship and non-self-governing territories. The British have come closest to accepting them as a general standard to guide future European-African relations.

OVER THE PAST TEN YEARS, THE AFRICA-ASIA BLOC IN the United Nations, and particularly the groups newly independent, have used every line of the Charter in an effort to bring the problems of colonial Africa before the United Nations. Of the 54 items on the agenda of the 1955 session of the General Assembly, 15 dealt with colonial issues and all except one of these concerned

Africa. The colonial powers for the most part maintained that the problems involved were their internal affair and that the use of the United Nations as a forum served simply to incite nationalism.

Whether or not the tactics of the Africa-Asia bloc are always justified, it is fortunate that the United Nations is available as a forum in which nationalist aspirations can be expressed and furthered by persuasion. The United Nations can do little to influence the strength and urgency of African nationalism, but it can have considerable effect on the atmosphere in which problems generated by nationalism are approached.

In this sense the United Nations may be at least as valuable to the colonial powers in providing a safety valve for nationalist ambitions as it is to the African nationalists in providing a world platform from which to attract support. American policy should, I believe, welcome and strengthen in every legitimate and reasonable way the role the United Nations can play in helping Africa's revolution to reach its goals in a manner as just, peaceful, and responsible, as conditions permit.

The only machinery for direct action in the United Nations is the International Trusteeship system, which has limited responsibility for 16 per cent of the people who live in colonial Africa. The two most relevant objectives of the trusteeship system as stated in the Charter are as follows:

> "To promote the political, economic, social, and educational advancement of the inhabitants of the trust territories, and their progressive development towards self-government or independence as may be appropriate to the particular circumstances of each territory and its people, and the freely expressed wishes of the peoples con-

cerned, and as may be provided by the terms of each trusteeship agreement.

"To encourage respect for human rights and for fundamental freedom for all without distinction as to race, sex, language, or religion, and to encourage recognition of the interdependence of the peoples of the world."

Under the terms of the Charter we are committed, together with all other members of the United Nations, to carry out this mandate. The Trusteeship Council is given three functions by the Charter: first, to consider progress reports which nations administering trust territories are required to submit; second, to accept and examine petitions; and third, to provide for periodic visits to trust territories.

These trust territories consist of the colonies which Germany lost in the first World War and those which Italy and Japan lost in the second. Although other dependent territories may be voluntarily placed under the trusteeship system, no instance thus far has occurred. The fact that an international trusteeship system exists at all seems to be an unforeseen benefit of two world wars.

In the Charter we also find the Declaration Regarding Non-Self-Governing Territories which applies to all colonies not included under the Trusteeship Council. This statement commits United Nations members to a milder version of the aims of the trusteeship system. It includes an obligation to submit to the Secretary General "information of a technical nature," on conditions in dependent areas. In 1947, the General Assembly set up a Committee on Information from Non-Self-Governing Territories to examine these data.

Beyond this, there are the general provisions of the

Charter under which, at one time or another, the United Nations has discussed the political difficulties in Morocco, Tunisia, and Algeria, and the racial conflicts of South Africa. In the nonpolitical field are the Economic and Social Council and the specialized agencies.

This rather extensive machinery was set up by the United Nations as a primary means of communication and influence in dealing with Africa. What use has the United States made of it?

Generally speaking it may be said that our approach has been timid and inconsistent. On only one type of question have we seemed to have had a positive policy: support for inclusion of items in the agenda. Only on rare occasions have we challenged the right of the United Nations to discuss any matter. On *no* occasion have we agreed with the European powers that the mere discussion of a colonial problem constitutes interference in internal affairs. When we did oppose discussion, it was because of our conviction that a debate on the issue in question might be more destructive than helpful at that particular time.

This question of whether or not to include an item in the agenda is much more than a procedural detail. Open discussion is the foundation of the Assembly's power. However, on no other really important colonial issue, with the exception of the report on Tanganyika to the Trusteeship Council in April 1956, which I shall discuss later, have we openly opposed Britain or France. Our usual tactic has been to attempt to avoid trouble for ourselves by abstaining.

The membership of both the Trusteeship Council and the Committee on Information from Non-Self-Governing Territories is equally divided between administering authorities, that is, nations responsible for trust territories or nations holding dependencies, and nonadministering powers. However much we may deplore it, African issues before these and similar bodies tend to become polarized in terms of colonial versus anticolonial and, more disturbing still, colored Asians and Africans versus white Europeans.

We qualify as an administering power because of the former Japanese islands which we now hold as a trust, and because of Alaska, Hawaii, the Virgin Islands, and Samoa. The other administering powers, which are by definition colonial powers, almost invariably vote together on basic issues, generally in opposition to the nonadministering or anticolonial powers. Since this circumstance often makes our vote the decisive one, we have become the reluctant arbiters in what amounts to a kind of global class struggle. This means that here in particular our split personality is dramatized before all the world.

Clearly, United States policy in support of African aspirations in the United Nations should make full use of the unquestioned legal powers of the Trusteeship Council. The Council cannot coerce anyone, but its powers to get the facts are extensive, and its power to admonish is unlimited.

The requirement that each administering nation report, as the Charter puts it, "on the political, economic, social and educational *advancement* of the inhabitants" in their trust territories, has undoubtedly helped to improve conditions in the trust areas. The fact that visiting missions must be allowed to tour these territories and that the Council may examine petitions from their inhabitants has also had its effect. With these powers firmly established in the Trusteeship Council and freely used, there is little that can be hidden.

The visiting mission has been one of the most effective instruments of the Council. The present practice is to cover each territory every three years. Mission reports are transmitted to the Trusteeship Council for discussion and debate.

But reports based on a six to eight weeks' tour of a large territory have their limitations, and much can happen in three years. We might, therefore, support practical measures to make this function of the Trusteeship Council more effective. In some cases at least, the missions should extend their stay or increase the number of their visits; or a permanent Trusteeship Council mission or representative could be assigned to observe and report between visits. As I see it, this proposal should be presented to the administering powers, not as an attempt to interfere with their administration, but as a means of more effectively gathering information in which the Trusteeship Council has a proper interest and concern.

The administering powers have often criticized the Council and visiting missions for their failure to comprehend all the facts. In good conscience thus they could hardly oppose a proposal which would serve further to enlighten the Council. Resident observers would be members of the Secretariat of the Trusteeship Division and present at the discussion of the Council concerning their particular territory.

The United Nations Advisory Council, which has been stationed in Italian Somaliland to watch that area's progress toward independence, provides a precedent for resident observers in all trust territories. At the very least, the Trusteeship Council could offer to assign resident observers to those who wish them.

In the crucial information-gathering function of the

Trusteeship Council, petitioners representing the people of the trust territories have played a valuable role. Inevitably the question arises as to whether all who wish to be heard by the Council should be heard. Hard and fast rules cannot be prescribed. Usually, however, the quickest way of determining the bona fides of a petitioner is to hear what he has to say. It would seem wise for the United States to support a broad interpretation of the Council's right to hear petitioners.

Because we do not share the direct vested interest in Africa of the other administering powers on the Council, we are in a position to take a more objective view than they can take. Similarly our view may often be more dispassionate than that of the anticolonial nonadministering powers. Hundreds of issues come up before each session of the Trusteeship Council which concern the rights of petitioners, reports of visiting missions and recommendations concerning administration policy in the territories. These give us an opportunity to stand consistently for justice in day-to-day human situations and often to play the role of a friendly arbitrator.

An unforeseen threat to the trusteeship system is the growth of administrative combinations under which the governing of a trust territory contiguous to an unsupervised colony is integrated with the administrative machinery of the colony.

If the trust territory is as advanced as the colony, and if the colony happens to be moving steadily toward self-determination, the trust territory can move along with it. On the other hand, a colony less advanced than a neighboring trust territory plus an administering authority that is resisting self-government can readily frustrate the aims of the trusteeship system.

The most advanced example of this complicated problem is Togoland, the former German colony. After

World War I, the western third of Togoland, adjoining the Gold Coast, became a British mandate, and the eastern two-thirds, adjoining French West Africa, became a French mandate. These are now trust territories, with British Togoland part of an administrative union with the Gold Coast, and French Togoland part of an administrative union with French West Africa.

In British Togoland, a plebiscite supervised by the United Nations, the first to be held in a trust territory, was conducted in May 1956. The voters were asked to choose between integration with the Gold Coast or a continuation under British administration as a trusteeship colony.

Although the Gold Coast is on the threshold of independence, no such prospect is in sight for French West Africa. Should the British Togolanders choose to join with the Gold Coast now, or should they hold out for independence until they could achieve it as a unified nation, or as a state in an independent Gold Coast federation?

Eighty-two per cent of the electorate went to the polls to give their answer following a vigorous and often bitter campaign. Fifty-eight per cent voted for an immediate association with the Gold Coast. Forty-two per cent voted for the status quo. If the United Nations Assembly ratifies the results of this plebiscite it can remove from its agenda an old and troublesome item.

SECRETARY HULL'S FOURTH POINT, THE SETTING OF INDIvidual target dates for self-determination, offers the United States perhaps its best opportunity to encourage African support for an orderly, long-range program of colonial liquidation both inside the Trusteeship Council and in the non-self-governing areas.

A precedent was set for establishing such target dates when the General Assembly decided in 1950 that Libya should become independent in two years and Italian Somaliland in ten. The precedent, however, is legal and not political. These were territories belonging to a defeated enemy, and victorious allies were contending over them; the Russians were embarrassingly ready and anxious to assume the role of trustee.

The objections to an expansion of this principle among the administering powers appear to be deep-rooted. In 1952, when the General Assembly invited all administering authorities to report on the estimated "period of time" each trust territory would need to achieve self-government or independence, none accepted the invitation.

In 1954 the Assembly recommended that administering authorities increase the number of representative governmental bodies in the territories and the degree of African participation in them. The purpose was to speed the day when dates could be set on which their territories might achieve self-government or independence. This recommendation also went unheeded.

To embark on any course that may be construed by a substantial group of nations as coercion or a violation of the Charter will serve to weaken rather than strengthen the United Nations. Yet it is difficult to see how America can continue to refuse to take a forthright position on the self-determination of subject peoples.

No responsible government that honestly seeks orderly progress in Africa can advocate the hurly-burly liquidation of colonial rule. On the other hand, to accept without protest the withholding of self-government until frustrated nationalist mobs have made both orderly colonial government and a dignified withdrawal impossible is at least equally irresponsible. The folly of this course has been demonstrated in both Indochina and North Africa.

The carefully planned, step-by-step evolution from colonial rule to self-government advocated by Mr. Cordell Hull appears to be a rational and proven alternative. In 1934 the United States gave dominion status to the Philippines and agreed to full independence in a ten year period. This promise was kept, and today the Philippines is a stable, democratic nation and a respected ally and associate of the United States. Likewise, Italian Somaliland, as we have seen, is to receive self-government in 1960.

In both these instances the establishment of a reasonable time schedule had a remarkable psychological effect on both the people concerned and the colonial administrators. In Somaliland today there is amazingly little tension and suspicion. The Somalis are confident and the Italians coöperative. No ugly racism complicates the scene. The contrast in Kenya directly to the south is no less than striking.

Economic development with clearly defined objectives by means of three-, five-, or seven-year economic plans, is commonplace in underdeveloped countries. Sometimes the established targets are reached ahead of schedule, and sometimes there are obstacles which slow down the expected rate of progress. These targets simply provide a workable but flexible timetable against which to organize the nation's resources to achieve a given economic objective.

This same approach, combining both economic and political targets, may offer the most practical approach to the orderly evolution of self-government in much of Africa. One thing is certain: unless progress toward

119

self-government goes hand-in-hand with economic development, there can be no lasting stability.

Although the variation from territory to territory would be great, the logical first goal might be improved local self-government within, say, five years. The program for this period might include school building, road building, and participation by Africans in simple advisory committees to encourage a growing reliance on local initiative and decision-making. For a brief trial period after the grant of local self-government, a veto power may be retained at a higher governmental level.

The second five-year plan in a given territory might have as its political objective *provincial* self-government with the veto power maintained for a trial period by the central government. The steps toward national self-government and ultimate independence could move from a national multiracial constituent assembly to self-government in all domestic affairs based on national multiracial assemblies, and finally to full-fledged self-determination with a common voting eligibility roll regardless of race.

The risks involved in the target-date system are by no means unreal, and the arguments against it will be supported by many earnest and liberal-minded men. There is always the possibility of unforeseen events. A target date which seemed reasonable when it was set may have to be postponed for legitimate reasons. If this occurs, confidence is shaken and old suspicions and frustrations increased.

If the date chosen is too far distant, nationalist groups would charge that the plan is one more delaying tactic; if it was so short-range as to create impossible targets, it would make an uneasy situation worse.

These difficulties are formidable but they do not seem

to me decisive. If progress lags behind the schedule, the schedule would have to be adjusted. If the reasons for the lag are honest miscalculations, and if the African nationalist leaders have a part in step-by-step development of the program, in most instances it would probably be accepted in good grace.

The United Nations process is an open one. The considerations that go with the setting of target dates will be there for all men to examine.

In spite of our own encouraging experience in the Philippines, the United States in the post-war years hesitated to press the administering nations toward a similar program calling for specific dates when independence might be possible. In January, 1955, this policy appeared to have been reversed. The American member of a United Nations visiting mission to Tanganyika on his own initiative joined with two other members to recommend that Britain be asked by the General Assembly to set a target date of 25 years for Tanganyika's independence. His vote created the necessary majority.

At that time I was visiting in Entebbe in the nearby British protectorate of Uganda. Here, as elsewhere in Africa, our unexpected action was greeted enthusiastically by African leaders. Yet, later in the year, when this recommendation came before the Trusteeship Council, our harried delegate, now acting as a representative of his government, was directed by the Department of State to vote against it.

On April 2, 1956, our position appeared again to have been reversed. Although the American delegate opposed "long-range time limits," he offered measured support for the setting of "intermediate targets for political as well as economic, social and educational advancement." Such targets he believed could give "a sense of purpose

121

and direction to the peoples who are on their way to the final goal."

Does this represent a fundamental switch in American policy on one of the most critical issues in African development, or was it a tactical and limited move? As this is written the point remains in doubt. But it was an immensely hopeful change nonetheless.

On this question, as on others, our use of the United Nations machinery in dealing with Africa should be not only imaginative and liberal, but objective. We must at all times take into account its limitations. In our advocacy of freedom we should not be tempted into irresponsibility. The African is the underdog. But he is not always right. Nor is the colonial power always wrong.

A particularly ticklish question involves jurisdiction. The Charter specifically forbids United Nations intervention "in matters which are essentially within the domestic jurisdiction of any state." Lawyers, of course, will never agree on where the line can be drawn between domestic and international affairs.

The soundest approach seems to me the pragmatic one. The United Nations is not a world government; it is a voluntary association of nations, as the Soviet Union, France, and the Union of South Africa have demonstrated by walking out of it at will. Pressure on the European powers that drives them to discard United Nations machinery or that arouses right-wing fears of world government, however hollow, will not further the objectives which we are striving to achieve.

One thing at least is certain: colonialism cannot be ignored as a political problem, it finds its way into almost every organ of the United Nations. For five years, for instance, the Commission on Human Rights has been torn by a controversy over whether the Covenant on Human Rights should include an article on self-determination, what the article, if any, should say, and whether it should apply to colonial areas. The treatment of Asian minorities in South Africa and the awesome crisis in race relations there have also been the subject of fruitless General Assembly efforts.

In the areas of nonpolitical development, the Economic and Social Council and all the specialized agencies have done worthwhile, although limited, work in Africa, and their activities should be expanded. A United Nations Economic Commission for Africa similar to the economic commissions now in existence for Europe, Latin America, and Asia could make an important contribution.

The United Nations Expanded Programme of Technical Assistance has a potentially important role to play. Yet largely because of the resistance of the colonial powers to foreign missions, less than 10 per cent of its resources have been allocated to this vast continent. Most of this goes to three independent nations, Liberia, Ethiopia, and Libya with a total population of less than 15,-000,000.

Of course the United States deals with Egypt, Ethiopia, Libya, Liberia, and the Union of South Africa as sovereign nations. Our direct relations with the Sudan, the Gold Coast, Nigeria, Somaliland, Morocco, and Tunisia which are in various stages of consolidating or anticipating independence, may soon be on the same basis. We have a special responsibility toward these independent countries with which we can negotiate bilateral economic-aid agreements. The needs of Tunisia and Morocco will be particularly urgent.

There is no space in this small book for a comprehensive discussion of foreign economic aid. Let me say again, however, that today modern Africa is primarily an economic, political, and ideological problem, or, more accurately, a series of problems. It will become a *military* problem only if we fail to meet this varied and immediate challenge.

In the expanded global economic effort that is so tragically long overdue, we should, I believe, include a substantial sum for economic assistance to African peoples whether subject or free. There should be no *political* strings, but to all our grants and loans we should apply constructive *administrative* conditions, among them the proviso that responsibility for economic progress must be accepted as far as possible by the people themselves.

In this way our economic effort can assist in seeking out and developing local, provincial, and national leadership. Let us have the courage frankly to inform our European associates that a primary purpose of our economic aid is to further orderly and responsible progress toward the ultimate freedom of the African in Africa. By so doing we will underscore our confidence in the future of free and viable African nations.

To identify ourselves, however indirectly, with the racial-economic discrimination that persists in rural colonial Africa will, of course, be disastrous. We should scrutinize each program carefully to make sure that it offers equal opportunities to persons of all races. Private American investors in Africa—whose investments now amount to nearly $300,000,000—can also help create confidence in our attitude and objectives by their own enlightened racial attitudes.

Europe's concern about the effects of political freedom for its African colonies on their own economies is legitimate. Yet the important adjustments which need to be made can only be made if the transition is peaceful.

America should let it be known that she is prepared

to ease the adjustment in both Africa and Europe by enlightened economic policies of her own. The traditional argument that the "loss" of colonies will inevitably lead to economic ruin is not borne out by the facts. Today the per-capita income of the Netherlands, in spite of the break with her former East Indian possessions, is among the highest in Europe. It is also instructive to compare the high per-capita incomes of Switzerland, Sweden, and Denmark, which have no overseas possessions, with that of Portugal, which is one of the four largest colonial powers.

WHEREVER WE CAN ESTABLISH CLOSER DIRECT CONTACT with the African people we should do so. I have been impressed with the earnestness and ability of most of our diplomatic and Point Four representatives whom I have met in Africa. But with few exceptions they are overworked and responsible for areas quite beyond their physical capacities. In all of *colonial* Africa, with a total population of 140,000,000 people, we have less than fifty American representatives, few of whom have a significant background in African affairs.

We should, I believe, assign more able American foreign-service people to Africa, give them a better background in African problems, and take greater pains to be certain that they are free of racial bias. It is particularly important to convince our representatives in Africa that their responsibilities are broader than their day-to-day contacts with the colonial governments. Of the four American consulates which I visited in colonial Africa in 1955, only one had ever had an African to dinner.

The selection of American representatives to staff the new embassies which I assume will soon be opened in Tunis and Rabat is vitally important.

In the State Department in Washington we need more people with special knowledge of Africa. Decision-making on African problems within the Department should be raised to higher levels.

Our information program in Africa should also be increased in size and broadened and improved in content. Most important of all, it should be directed to the Africans rather than to the thin crust of Europeans at the top.

Of the 680 book borrowers registered in 1955 in the United States Information Agency in Leopoldville, Belgian Congo, only 12 were Africans. The library contained 4,020 books in English; 280 in French. I asked how many people in Leopoldville could read or speak English. "Perhaps 1800, all but a few of them Belgians," was the answer. If the purpose of our information program in the Congo is to convince the Belgians, it would be more efficient to concentrate our efforts in Brussels.

We may hope that American foundations and universities will steadily increase their interest and activities in Africa. Here again, as in the State Department, progress is often handicapped by a lack of trained people. At present, there are only three well established centers of African studies in the United States—at Boston University, Howard University, and Northwestern. Although each is making an excellent contribution to our steadily growing understanding of Africa, the continent is vast and they can do little more than scratch the surface. In this field of special international studies, as in so many others, the Russians are now outdistancing us.

Particularly vital and also rather ticklish is increased exchange of students and community leaders. Many of Africa's most promising leaders south of the Sahara, as we have seen, are graduates of American universities. In addition to Kwame Nkrumah and Dr. Nnamdi Azikiwe, there are Dr. Hastings Banda of Nyasaland, Peter Mbiyu Koinange of Kenya, Dr. E. Kalibala of Uganda, and many others.

Cultural interchange in a variety of fields is badly needed. Africans generally have a great interest in America—interests which range from a spiritual and intellectual affinity with our faiths and our anticolonial history to curiosity about the success which so many American Negroes have achieved in business, the professions, and the arts and our jazz music. Louis "Satchmo" Armstrong played to an audience of 100,000 dancing, shouting Gold Coasters on his brief visit there in May 1956.

The mere presence in Africa of outstanding American Negroes as musicians, lecturers, teachers, performers, students, will do everyone concerned a world of good.

It goes without saying that the position of the Negro in American life is crucial to our relations with Africa and adds a new difficult dimension to our exchange program. But in spite of increased tensions in some areas our position in general is far stronger than it was ten years ago and we should not hesitate to treat the problems that remain with complete frankness.

If in our direct personal relations with Africans in the United Nations, and, indeed, in the totality of our American policy we are able to persuade Africans that we as a people favor their independence as quickly as they can manage it responsibly, we will be in a position to perform a uniquely useful service. Once we are trusted we can often help moderate the impatience of those Africans who want more authority than they are yet able to use constructively.

Experience has persuasively demonstrated that a stubborn effort by the European powers to cling to colonial advantages will only increase the force of the eventual explosion, and if we appear even by indirection to support the European dominated status quo, much of the bitter resentment will be directed against us. Yet indiscriminate and reckless support of African nationalism would in many areas encourage the very conflicts we are most anxious to avoid by setting Islam against Christianity, tribal areas against cities, Berbers against Arabs, Indians against Bantus, and all of them against the Europeans.

Britain, France, Portugal, and Belgium still control three-fourths of Africa. We must face the fact that what these four colonial powers do in Africa in the next decade will have a greater effect on the course of events than what we do. Indeed, in much of Africa, whatever we accomplish in the next decade will be largely within the context of continuing European authority or under its direct auspices.

Our efforts to persuade our Atlantic associates to adopt a more liberal and flexible approach will require an especially large measure of tact and understanding. There will be occasions when frank and even blunt language may be called for. Yet pompous lectures to our European friends by American leaders, regardless of the applause they may win from the Africans, are more likely to set back the cause of orderly and responsible self-government than to advance it.

We have no monopoly of anticolonial virtue. Many Europeans—possibly most of them—agree that a new age is dawning in Africa and that the Atlantic nations have a responsibility for speeding that day. Ideals of freedom, though dramatized for the anticolonial world by our own revolution, were ideals which germinated in

Britain and France. Let us approach Europe, therefore, unhampered by any smug vision of stereotyped imperialist villainy, and attune our policies and aspirations to the liberal, not the reactionary, leaders of Europe.

However, our European associates should recognize our right not only to speak, but to act on African problems. Basic to the NATO alliance is the assumption that the Atlantic nations face common problems which can best be met by common action based on a common awareness of the challenge of today's new world.

Britain is the only colonial power which fully accepts the principle of self-determination for its African colonies. The Portuguese bluntly reject self-rule in its entirety. The French and the Belgians have their own special reservations based on the complex attitudes I have described.

Thus on many questions we will be tempted to withdraw, to express privately our disappointment over the narrow outlook of our NATO associates, to suggest that this view may ultimately lead to another costly colonial debacle, and finally to decide uneasily that the safest course is one of silence and inaction. But to take this negative path means to abdicate our position of responsibility and leadership and grant to our allies the power of veto over American policy in this crucial continent, and indirectly over our relations with the Asian nations as well.

If there is anything clear in Africa by this time, it is the relentless pressure of the forces which we have been discussing, in the forefront of which stands ardent nationalism against the explosive background of racial tensions and suspicions. The stubborn inability of the Atlantic powers to understand the power of this combination has led us from setback to setback.

If the French had learned from Chiang Kai-shek's abject failure in China, they could have saved thousands of lives, much treasure, and their own prestige in Indochina. Yet there the same costly mistakes were repeated. And now the lessons have had to be learned all over again in North Africa.

America bears its share of responsibility for these developments. To be sure, we warned our French friends in private that colonial military power based on a corrupt, landlord-ridden feudalism could not defeat the nationalist movement, the leadership of which they had allowed the Communists to capture. Still, we bet $3,000,-000,000 in military equipment, or three times our total world-wide investment in Point Four, that the French with all their mistakes could somehow hold Vietnam against the Communist forces. We lost the bet and the world knows we lost it.

We can be sure that the remaining colonial peoples of Africa will demand independence before most Western students of government believe they are ready for it. Many educated, responsible Africans say frankly that they would prefer to govern themselves inefficiently and corruptly than to be governed with efficiency and honesty by European foreigners. The fanatics put it more strongly: if forced to choose, they would take their chances with anarchy and a return to raw tribalism.

We must face the fact that as new African nations become independent the level of government efficiency will almost certainly go down. The best that outsiders can do is to help hold the depreciation within reasonable limits. The best possible balance must be struck between the necessary minimum of economic and political advancement and experience, on the one hand, and pressures for independence on the other.

We have seen that the pattern in much of Africa has been one of nationalist threat followed by European counterthreat, followed by riots, followed by conference, followed by grudging concessions to the nationalists, followed by a temporary truce, after which the costly and embittering cycle is repeated. Indeed this has been the classic cycle in the break-up of empires throughout history.

Perhaps in the final hour of European empire in Africa this pattern may be changed. The concessions are inevitable, but begrudging and bitter they need not be. Indeed what are now concessions could become agreed landmarks on the road to freedom along which Europeans, instead of being dragged, could travel hand in hand with the Africans.

Many will suggest that the orderly evolutionary approach which I have proposed is a practical impossibility. Their judgment may indeed prove to be correct. But if so, the Atlantic powers will meet with a series of debacles in Africa which are even more clearly foreseeable than the costly setbacks which have already occurred in China, Indochina, and the Middle East.

As this is written in May, 1956, the outlook for a fresh approach to Africa in the near future does not appear bright. America still seems to be adrift without a policy and without even a clear objective. Proposals for action, however reasonable, are promptly cancelled out by proposals equally persuasive for waiting and seeing.

As long as this sterile mood continues to paralyze us, we will remain as diplomatically incapable of dealing with Soviet Cold War tactics between Tokyo and Capetown as we would be militarily incapable if the Soviet Union alone possessed nuclear weapons.

Yet it would be escapist to assume that the Soviet

Union alone is responsible for our present difficulties. In large measure these difficulties have grown out of the extraordinary technological changes of our time, compounded by our own blunders, our own timidity, our own insensibility to the new realities of power. Much of the ground that the Communists have gained in Asia and Africa may be credited to the skill with which they have capitalized on American mistakes and the tact and vigor with which they have pressed their own versions of Point Four and cultural exchange.

There is no reason, however, to resort to panicky, expedient action, or to lose confidence in the final outcome. The Atlantic nations alone can offer Africans what they want most desperately—peaceful as opposed to violent change. What is needed is a calm, considered reappraisal of our position, a fresh approach dealing with all aspects of our African relations, political, military, economic, and ideological, and a series of moves designed to dramatize our objectives.

If we alone or with the British should propose a charter for Africa based on those five key principles of Cordell Hull, the result in Asia as well as Africa would be electric, and we would move far toward recapturing the initiative which we have lost.

In principle the colonial powers are already committed under the Charter of the United Nations to promote the self-government and welfare of their dependent people. Yet the kind of charter which I suggest for Africa would go beyond a statement of principles to include a proposal for the evolution of self-government through coördinated economic and political development on the basis of an attainable timetable.

Such a charter would provide a new practical meaning to the principles and values on which Western civilization was based in a world which is yearning for the triumph of reason over violence, and for an effective reassertion of the rights of man. Let me add one warning: *we had better mean what we say.*

No one who has read thus far will infer that the challenge we face in Africa is a simple one that will respond quickly to good will, money, and new slogans. On the contrary, we have here a series of situations which involve vigorously supported and often opposed economic and political interests, operating within an outmoded colonial framework which is often heavily charged with racial emotions, all under the unrelenting pressure of a timetable which is no longer subject to control by even the most reasonable men.

The following central questions on the African agenda are momentous, and no responsible man will attempt to predict the answers:

In the independent and about-to-be-independent African nations, can some effective form of democracy survive the pressures of sectional and tribal differences, administrative inexperience, and often impossible demands for rapid economic progress?

Can some miracle bring a measure of enlightenment to the South African nationalists sufficient to avoid what appears to be an inevitable explosion or, failing that, can the explosion be limited to South Africa?

Can the British Colonial Office and the more responsible white settlers of British East and Central Africa loosen the grip of the die-hards and forge a true multiracial partnership before the situation there gets out of hand? Can similar statesmanship save the day in Algeria?

Can progress toward self-government generally strike a compromise between the dual danger of unreasonable delay and precipitous action, both of which play into the hands of the most destructive and irresponsible elements both within Africa and elsewhere?

The answers to these decisive questions are in themselves largely dependent on the willingness of the colonial powers to recognize the inevitability of African self-determination and to accept the fact that only the pace, method, and cost remain in question.

America's role will be determined by her ability to shake loose from her present negative fascination with what *Moscow* is doing, avoid panicky action, and apply her influence and resources toward the responsible solution of the problems that constitute the African dilemma.

This latter proposition, of course, can only be approached within the large framework of American foreign policy throughout the world. Here we must express the fervent hope that we shall soon come to view the Soviet challenge not negatively as a mortal danger, but positively as an opportunity for which the continuing political, social, and industrial revolution of Jefferson, Lincoln, and Henry Ford has equipped us as no other people on earth.

In that direction alone can we rediscover our own traditional sense of national purpose and thus rededicate our energies to the only objective which will give us common cause with a majority of mankind—the pursuit of freedom, opportunity, dignity, and peace for all men everywhere.